First World War
and Army of Occupation
War Diary
France, Belgium and Germany

41 DIVISION
Divisional Troops
Royal Army Medical Corps
138 Field Ambulance
3 May 1916 - 31 October 1917

WO95/2628/1

The Naval & Military Press Ltd
www.nmarchive.com
Published in association with The National Archives

Published by

The Naval & Military Press Ltd

Unit 10 Ridgewood Industrial Park,

Uckfield, East Sussex,

TN22 5QE England

Tel: +44 (0) 1825 749494

www.naval-military-press.com

www.nmarchive.com

This diary has been reprinted in facsimile from the original. Any imperfections are inevitably reproduced and the quality may fall short of modern type and cartographic standards.

© **Crown Copyright**
Images reproduced by permission of The National Archives, London, England, 2015.

Contents

Document type	Place/Title	Date From	Date To
Heading	WO95/2628-1		
Heading	41st Division 138th Fld Ambulance May 1916-Oct 1917 Mar 1918-1919 May Italy 1917 Nov-1918 Feb.		
Heading	War Diary Of 138 Field Ambulance R.A.M.C. From 3-5-1916. To 31-5-1916. Vol 1.		
War Diary	Le Havre	03/05/1916	04/05/1916
War Diary	Loolwarrvelde.	05/05/1916	05/05/1916
War Diary	Strazeele	05/05/1916	09/05/1916
War Diary	Sheet 36 A.15.C.75.	09/05/1916	28/05/1916
War Diary	Steenwerck.	29/05/1916	31/05/1916
Heading	War Diary Of 138th Field Ambulance R.A.M.C. From 1st June 1916 To 30th June 1916 Vol. 2.		
War Diary	Steenwerck.	01/06/1916	30/06/1916
Heading	War Diary Of 138th Field Ambulance R.A.M.C. From July 1-1916 To July 31-1916 (Volume 3).		
War Diary	Steenwerck.	01/07/1916	31/07/1916
Heading	War Diary Of 138th Field Ambulance R.A.M.C. From August 1st 1916 To August 31st 1916 (Volume 4).		
War Diary	Steenwerck.	01/08/1916	17/08/1916
War Diary	Fletre.	18/08/1916	24/08/1916
War Diary	Bouchon.	25/08/1916	31/08/1916
Heading	War Diary Of 138th Field Amb 41st Divisional from 1st September to 30th September 1916 (Volume V).		
War Diary	Bouchon.	01/09/1916	01/09/1916
War Diary	Ailly Le h Clocher Area.	02/09/1916	05/09/1916
War Diary	Dernacourt Area. Map 62D E.15.a.5.10.	06/09/1916	09/09/1916
War Diary	Sheet 62D.	10/09/1916	13/09/1916
War Diary	F.6.a.20.	10/09/1916	17/09/1916
War Diary	Sheet 62D E.15.a.	18/09/1916	20/09/1916
War Diary	Buirre D.23.c.71.	22/09/1916	30/09/1916
Heading	War Diary 138th Field Amb October 1916 Vol 6 41st Div.		
War Diary	S.16.c.94	11/10/1916	11/10/1916
War Diary	F.8.C.	12/10/1916	12/10/1916
War Diary	Boirre D.23.C.71.	13/10/1916	24/10/1916
War Diary	Wippenhoeck	24/10/1916	01/11/1916
Heading	War Diary Of 138th Field Ambulance. From:- November 1st 1916. To:- November 30th 1916. (Volume VII.) 41st Div.		
War Diary	Wippenhoeck.	02/11/1916	30/11/1916
Heading	War Diary Of 138th Field Ambulance R.A.M.C. From 1st December 1916 To December 31st 1916. (Volume VIII.) 41st Div.		
War Diary	Wippenhoek.	01/12/1916	31/12/1916
Heading	War Diary Of 138th Field Ambulance R.A.M.C. From Jan. 1st 1917 To Jan 31st 1917. (Volume 9.)		
War Diary	Wippenhoek.	01/01/1917	09/01/1917
War Diary	Renninghelst	10/01/1917	31/01/1917

Heading	War Diary Of 138th Field Ambulance From 1st February 1917 To February 28th 1917 (Volume 2.) 41st Div.		
War Diary	Renninghelst.	01/02/1917	28/02/1917
Heading	War Diary Of 138th Field Ambulance From March 1st To March 31st 1917. (Volume III) 41st Div.		
War Diary	Renninghelst.	01/03/1917	31/03/1917
Heading	War Diary Of 138th Field Ambulance From 1st April 1917, To 30th April 1917 (Volume IV).		
War Diary		01/04/1917	16/04/1917
War Diary	Renninghelst.	17/04/1917	30/04/1917
Heading	War Diary Of 138th Field Ambulance From May 1st To May 31st 1917. (Volume V.).		
War Diary	Renninghelst.	01/05/1917	31/05/1917
Heading	War Diary Of 138th Field Ambulance R.A.M.C. From:- June 1st 1917. To:- June 30th 1917. Volume VI.		
Miscellaneous	Appendix "C" Limber No. 2.		
Map	Appendix "D".		
War Diary	Reninghelst.	01/06/1917	05/06/1917
War Diary	Quderdom 9.30.c.48.	06/06/1917	08/06/1917
War Diary	Quderdom.	08/06/1917	13/06/1917
War Diary	Hallebast Corner (28.S.W. N.3.d.3.8.)	13/06/1917	15/06/1917
War Diary	Hallebast Corner.	16/06/1917	22/06/1917
War Diary	Nr La Clytte N.1.d.2.2.	22/06/1917	30/06/1917
Miscellaneous	Appendix "C" Minimum Equipment For An Advanced Dressing Station. Limber No.1.		
Operation(al) Order(s)	138th Field Ambulance. R.A.M.C. Operation Order No. 4. Appendix "A".	04/06/1917	04/06/1917
Miscellaneous	Appendix "A" Special Duties N.C.O's and men.		
Miscellaneous	Appendix "B".		
Miscellaneous	Appendix "B" War Diary Volume VI. Page 2 Report On Operation 7th. June-8th. June 1917.	07/06/1917	07/06/1917
Heading	War Diary Of 138th Field Ambulance R.A.M.C. From:- July 1st 1917 To:- July 31st 1917. (Volume VII).		
War Diary	Nr Fletre Sheet 27. S.E W.5.c.3.9.	01/07/1917	14/07/1917
War Diary	Sheet 27 S.E W.5.C.3.9	15/07/1917	23/07/1917
War Diary	Sheet 28 S.W. M.3.C.2.1/2.8.	23/07/1917	24/07/1917
War Diary	Sheet 27 S.E. R.10.a.3.3 Boeschepe.	25/07/1917	26/07/1917
War Diary	Sheet 27 R.10.a.3.3 Boeschepe.	28/07/1917	31/07/1917
Operation(al) Order(s)	138th Field Ambulance Operation Order No. 5. Appendix "C".	11/06/1917	11/06/1917
Operation(al) Order(s)	138th. Field Ambulance Operation Order No. 6. Appendix "D".	13/06/1917	13/06/1917
Miscellaneous	Appendix "E". Report On Operations Of The 14th., inst.	15/06/1917	15/06/1917
Operation(al) Order(s)	138th Field Ambulance Operation Order No. 7. Appendix "F".	25/06/1917	25/06/1917
Heading	War Diary of the 138th Field Ambulance. From August 1st 1917 Till August 31st 1917. (Volume VIII).		
War Diary	Boeschepe Sheet 27 S.E. R.10.a.3.3.	01/08/1917	25/08/1917
War Diary	Staple Area.	26/08/1917	26/08/1917
War Diary	Cormette Sheet 27a Q.34.a.5.5.	27/08/1917	31/08/1917
Heading	War Diary Of 138th, Field Ambulance. September 1st. 1917-September 30th 1917. (Volume IX).		
War Diary	Cormette Sheet 27 A S.E Q.34.a.5.5.	01/09/1917	07/09/1917
War Diary	Cormette Camp Q.34.a.5.5. Sheet 27 A.S.E.	07/09/1917	14/09/1917

War Diary	Wallon Cappel Area Sheet 27 O 30.b.7.5.	14/09/1917	15/09/1917
War Diary	Boeschepe Sheet 27. S.E. R.10.a.3.3.	15/09/1917	25/09/1917
War Diary	Boeschepe R.10.a.3.3. Sheet 27 S.E.	19/09/1917	26/09/1917
War Diary	Leffrinckoucke C.5.a.5.5 Sheet 19.	27/09/1917	27/09/1917
War Diary	La. Panne, Sheet XI W.20.b.7.9.	28/09/1917	28/09/1917
War Diary	La Panne.	29/09/1917	30/09/1917
Heading	War Diary Of 138th Field Ambulance From:- October 1st 1917. To:- October 31st 1917. (Volume X).		
War Diary	La Panne W.20.b.7.6 Sheet 11 S.E.	01/10/1917	01/10/1917
War Diary	La Panne.	02/10/1917	06/10/1917
War Diary	Oost Dunkerke Bains R.27.c.55.56 Sheet XI S.E.	06/10/1917	11/10/1917
War Diary	Oost Dunkerke Bains R.27.c.55.26 Sheet XI.	12/10/1917	29/10/1917
War Diary	Uxem Sheet XIX I.6.a.29.	29/10/1917	31/10/1917

W005/2629(1)

41ST DIVISION

138TH FLD AMBULANCE
MAY 1916-~~DEC 1918~~ OCT 1917
MAR 1918 — 1919 MAY

ITALY 1917 NOV — 1918 FEB

41ST DIVISION

138 F Amb
Vol 1

4ld R.

May 19th

CONFIDENTIAL

War Diary

of

138 Field Ambulance R.A.M.C.

From 3-5-1916.   To. 31-5-1916.

Dec 18

COMMITTEE FOR THE
MEDICAL HISTORY OF THE WAR
Date 26 JUN 1915

WAR DIARY
INTELLIGENCE SUMMARY
(Erase heading not required.)

Army Form C. 2118

Instructions regarding War Diaries and Intelligence Summaries are contained in F.S. Regs., Part II. and the Staff Manual respectively. Title Pages will be prepared in manuscript.

Place	Date	Hour	Summary of Events and Information	Remarks and references to Appendices
Le Havre	2.5.16	9.30am	Disembarked from "H.M.T. Viper." Apportioning major R. Pine	2/1
		11.00	Remainder Rest of amb. (4 Officers, 19 R. amb. rank ASC personnel with Horses Transport) disembarked from "Australind"	2/1
"		15.30	Proceeded to No. 2 Rest Camp.	2/1
"	4.5.16	9.30	Left Rest Camp for Station.	2/1
"		14.30	After entraining (rather troublesome owing to size of loading of transport) left Le Havre	2/1
Godewaersvelde	5.5.16	12.0 noon	Detrained. Marched to STRAZEELE via FLETRE. Weather was fair en route. Weather very hot.	2/1
Strazeele	"	17.30	Arrived in Billets # 1 kilom. S.W. of STRAZEELE. Billetted in 2 farm houses - (also farm - 3 officers being in STRAZEELE - men in barns - Transport (horses in fields near lower farm - water fed at lower farm, worked at up/per.	2/1
	6.5.16		Opened tent section & received sick from 122 & 123 Inf. Bdes.	2/1
	7.5.16		2 motor amb. wagons lent from II Corp for inspection pending arrival of M.T. Move orders received 23 hrs.	2/1
	8.5.16		Weather fine, showery.	2/1
	9.5.16		O.C. + Motor Officers to IX + XVII Div.s for 3 days instruction. O.C. + 2 Offrs to 28 F. Amb. + 2 Offrs to XVII Div.	2/1
Sheet 36 A 15 C 75	10	12	F. Amb. marched at 12 Noon to LE KIRLEM (Kitchen farm. Map sheet 36 A 15 C 75. (Another LE KIRLEM is in A 22 Reforming 122 Infy Bde Area	2/1
	10.5.16		Sick of no Duty Bde. evacuated to HAZEBROUCK.	2/1
	11.5.16		Motor transport to arrive tomorrow	2/1
	12.5.16		O.C. + 4 Offrs returned. Capt Lowder + 3 Offrs went on course of instruction. Motor Transport arrived 11 hrs.	2/1

1875 Wt. W593/826 1,000,000 4/15 J.B.C. & A. A.D.S.S./Forms/C. 2118.

WAR DIARY
or
INTELLIGENCE SUMMARY
(Erase heading not required.)

Army Form C. 2118

Instructions regarding War Diaries and Intelligence Summaries are contained in F.S. Regs., Part II. and the Staff Manual respectively. Title Pages will be prepared in manuscript.

Place	Date	Hour	Summary of Events and Information	Remarks and references to Appendices
	13.5.16		Wet day. Orders for move received (secret)	a/w
	14.5.16		Move postponed.	a/w
	15.5.16		3 Officers away for instructional purposes returned.	a/w
	16.5.16		Capt. Binney & Lieut. Hutson to the left for instructions with 28th Div.	a/w
	17.5.16		Another air alarm at 23 hrs. 15 men stood to for ½ hr.	
	18.5.16		News received at 3 a.m. of gas attack warning. sent off at 11.30 am. No gas here.	a/w
	19.5.16		A.D.M.S. visited 7 A. Orders received in event of a move. 25 men under Sergt. McIntosh sent to strengthen New A.D.S. on L sector.	a/w
	20.5.16		Capt. Binney & instruction party returned. Div. R.9. opened at (Austin) CAESTRE	a/w
	21.5.16		Instructional party sent to A.D.S. & New A.D.S. 2 O/s 24 O.A.	a/w
	22.5.16		Nothing to report. Another inst. party to A.D.S.	a/w
	23.5.16		Move received. Another inst. party to A.D.S.	a/w
	24.5.16		Reveillé time table. Air raid alarm 11.30 p.m. Another Inst. Party	a/w
	25.5.16		Off. & ex-Division Ol Sanitary appliances.	a/w
	26.5.16		Officers & Storm returned for works on A.D.S. Equipment of 1 section sent in to 29 F.A. at STEENWERCK + 3 O.R. proceeded no advance party to take over from 29 F.A.	a/w
	27.5.16		Three officers T. 3 & Adv. Binney Str near PLOEGSTEERT. Started obtaining fuel stores for works.	a/w
	28.5.16		Visited A.D.S. + from 112 Inf.y. Adv. at 12.20 a.m. When inspected no 6 helmets. The gas arrived then alert received from orders received accelerator movement. 11.30 p.m.	a/m
STEENWERCK	29.5.16	7 am	30th am Main division St.a. from 29 F.A. Ands. at STEENWERCK. Visited A.D.S. which was under a halfstop for about 1½ hrs this morning. One man slightly wounded. Visited new A.D.S. which though not finished is capable of being used if old A.D.S. becomes too hot.	a/m
	30.5.16		Visited A.D.S. + New A.D.S. work proceeding satisfactorily	a/m
	31.6.16		drew materials for shell proof shelter for new A.D.S. Usual orders for medical arrangements in case of attack by enemy.	

A. Williams
Major R.A.M.C.

138 F Amb
Vol 2
June

CONFIDENTIAL.

WAR DIARY

OF

138th FIELD AMBULANCE R.A.M.C.

FROM 1st JUNE 1916   TO   30th JUNE 1916

VOL. 2.

COMMITTEE FOR THE
MEDICAL HISTORY OF THE WAR
Date 5 AUG. 1916

WAR DIARY
or
INTELLIGENCE SUMMARY
(Erase heading not required.)

Army Form C. 2118

Instructions regarding War Diaries and Intelligence Summaries are contained in F.S. Regs., Part II. and the Staff Manual respectively. Title Pages will be prepared in manuscript.

Place	Date	Hour	Summary of Events and Information	Remarks and references to Appendices
STEENWERCK	1-6-16		Proceeded to site of Divisional Collecting station for walking wounded (If such should be required) and instructed M.O. i/c Div. Train & Sanitary Section, who are detailed for it, in the necessary dispositions.	A/Lieut Major Rowe
	2-6-16		Nothing to report.	A/W
	3-6-16		Relieved half the A.D.S. party. In future half will be relieved on Wednesdays.	A/W
	4-6-16		Plat/for Sato.	A/W
	5-6-16		G.O.C. 91 Div visited F.A. D.D.M.S. visited. Visited A.D.S. new A.D.S.	A/W
	7-6-16		Visited A.D.S.	A/W
	10-6-16		Orders received for fatigue party tomorrow for new R.A.P. Left Exeter.	A/W
	13-6-16		Examined country to left of present position with a view to selecting new A.D.S. if it should be necessary. Blankets all but 25% taken in from personnel.	A/W
	14-6-16		Time changed to my W. clocks put 1 hr forward at 11 P.M.	A/W
	15-6-16		The weather for the past fortnight has been extremely cold, windy, & a good deal of rain.	A/W
	16-6-16	12 Noon	General Gas Alert received from 122 Inf. Bde.	A/W
	17-6-16	12·37 a.m.	Gas Alarm Dr. Do. All precautions taken. No gas came to M.D.S. but at A.D.S. helmets had to be worn for about an hour. One case of gassing occurred & was evacuated. No cases in Amb. personnel.	A/W

Army Form C. 2118

WAR DIARY
or
INTELLIGENCE SUMMARY
(Erase heading not required.)

Instructions regarding War Diaries and Intelligence Summaries are contained in F.S. Regs., Part II. and the Staff Manual respectively. Title Pages will be prepared in manuscript.

Place	Date	Hour	Summary of Events and Information	Remarks and references to Appendices
STEEN-WERCK	18.6.16	11.55p	Gas alarm of view. No gas arrived at either MDS or A.D.S. No casualties	a/w
	19.6.16		Half fatigue party from R.A.P. withdrawn to finish work on new A.D.S.	a/w
	21.6.16		Sanitary Officer II Army visited main dressing station.	a/w
	22.6.16		Strained vicinity of NIEPPE with a view to future site for M.D.S.	a/w
	23.6.16		"Gas alarm from South" received 12.30 a.m. from 132 Inft Bde. No gas arrived in this area.	a/w
	24.6.16		Visited PLOEGSTEERT vicinity to work for new A.D.S. Settled on U.19.c.9.6.	a/w
			Withdrew 6 men from work party on new A.D.S. Lt. Oliver proceeded to 12th E. Surrey Regt. to bring up 7 W	
	25.6.16			
	26.6.16		Received working parties 25 from 140th & 60 from 139th when with 25 men from this F.A. started	a/w
	27.6.16		work on new A.D.S. at Sheet 28 U.19/c.9.6	
	28.6.16		During last week weather has been fine but cold. Moderate rainfall except on 16th & 17th when it was N.E.ly. wind S.W.	
	29.6.16		Arranged with O/C A.D.S. to be in positions in case of increased activity. Two days action supplied this evening viz for 30th June & 1st July. Orders issued for all water receptacles to be full at 6 a.m. g.t.o. Parties withdrawn from various works. Personnel at Aid Posts doubled. 25 of works parties were left at new A.D.S. near Douoen Farm Premesoles brought to 2 ADS Qrs.	Offr.
	30.6.16	9.30pm	Lt J. Rueden R.A.M.C. arrived for duty. Orders received that we within (a raid would be made after bombardment & gas to start at 10 p.m.) A.D.S. informed.	

1875 Wt. W593/826 1,000,000 4/15 J.B.C. & A. A.D.S.S./Forms/C.2118.

a/Wilkinson
Major RAMC

41/ July Vol 3

CONFIDENTIAL.

War Diary

of

138th Field Ambulance R.A.M.C.

(Volume 3).

From July 1-1916   To July 31-1916

COMMITTEE FOR THE
MEDICAL HISTORY OF THE WAR
Date 5 – SEP. 1916

Army Form C. 2118

WAR DIARY
or
INTELLIGENCE SUMMARY
(Erase heading not required.)

Instructions regarding War Diaries and Intelligence Summaries are contained in F.S. Regs., Part II. and the Staff Manual respectively. Title Pages will be prepared in manuscript.

Place	Date	Hour	Summary of Events and Information	Remarks and references to Appendices
STEENWERCK	1-7-16		There were 58 admissions the result of last night's activities. Of these 20 were the result of our gas & of these 20 - 13 occurred in 3rd Bn Spec. R.E. 3c is sad that these were due to bursting of our cylinders by hostile fire but I have no proof of this. Working parties sent out again to carry on with construction of new A.D.S. under Lieut Sheldon R.E. who is look'g by 139 & 90 Amb. to supervise this work.	Mollusca Oranges Ham
	2.7.16		A party of 16 men v. 1 NCO sent out to work with similar parties from 139 to Y 140 & 7 A.S. also under Lieut Sheldon on making a new R.A.P. on LOWNDES AVENUE. Weather much warmer & Summerlike.	a/w.
	3.7.16		at U.27.c.18, 3 R.A.P. and this 7A took over R.A.P. at U.19.a.77 instead owing to modifications	a/w
	6.7.16		140th F.A. took over No. 3 R.A.P. from work party. Occupied Estaminet au Retour de la Chasse with drew 10 men & Sgt. from work party.	a/w.
	7.7.16		Sunn is at rate of New A.D.S. Started work on a new M.D.S. at NIEPPE. Took over from Ambases the A.D.S. in ROMARIN & occupied it	a/w
	8.7.16		Ordered doubling of F.A. personnel at R.A.P.s because of minor interference to night.	a/w
	9.7.16		These new frames were cancelled on acct of change of plans.	a/w.
	10.7.16		Conferences - decided to have 5000 dressings in reserve on burn W & bandages & oz wool & ½ yd gauze per dressing. Also to have 150 Statchers 190 Pailliasses & 410 Blankets on hand. Look stock & found 1540 Shell dressings, 2,250 Bandages & 2976 dressings and 2870 yds gauze = 5740 dressings. Indents for	a/w
	11.7.16 12.7.16		93 lbs of wool & 2976 dressings amounts to complete. Informed to day that Sd Establishment is reduced to M.T. 13. H.T. 38. Orders given to double personnel at R.A.P.s because of expected enemy retaliation tonight after a gas attack.	a/w. a/w
	13.7.16		Gas attack did not take place but there were some 30 casualties during the night because of enemy activity.	a/w.

Army Form C. 2118

WAR DIARY
or
INTELLIGENCE SUMMARY
(Erase heading not required.)

Instructions regarding War Diaries and Intelligence Summaries are contained in F.S. Regs., Part II. and the Staff Manual respectively. Title Pages will be prepared in manuscript.

Place	Date	Hour	Summary of Events and Information	Remarks and references to Appendices
STEENWERCK	14.7.16		Lieut Roche proceeded to Div.H. Train in Tempy Medical charge.	a/w
	15.7.16		Visited NIEPPE M.D.S. & found work progressing satisfactorily.	a/w
	16.7.16		Weather cold & wet. Wind changed to N.E. Gas alert ordered.	a/w
	17.7.16		A Shell landed beside Dressing Station ROMARIN. Broke many windows but no casualties among our men. Another shell landed near new A.D.S. at ESTAMINET À LA RETOUR DE LA CHASE.	a/w
	18.7.16		Work at LOWNDES AVE. interrupted by shell fire. Enemy seems frequently	a/w
	19.7.16		Gas alert ended. Wind veered to N.W.	a/w
	20.7.16		Horse killed at Romarin by German anti-aircraft shell (dud). A.D.M.S. inspected books of Field Ambs.	a/w
	21.7.16		Gas alert received 2.a.m. Lt. Roche returned to duty with F.Amb.	a/w
	22.7.16		Nil	a/w
	23.7.16		Nil	a/w
	24.7.16		Capt. A.E. KNIGHT Tempy. R.A.M.C. reported for temporary duty.	a/w
	25.7.16		122 Duffy Pass order 26 received. The R.Dr moving from L.of. our sector to L. of. the area on our right.	a/w
	26.7.16		Combined raid etc. carried out on the centre & left sectors. A.D.S. manned, 6 men sent to 140th F.A. A.D.S. for instruction as to their R.A.Ps & trenches.	a/w

1875 Wt. W593/826 1,000,000 4/15 T.R.C.&A. A.D.S.S./Forms/C. 2118.

Army Form C. 2118

WAR DIARY
or
INTELLIGENCE SUMMARY
(Erase heading not required.)

Instructions regarding War Diaries and Intelligence Summaries are contained in F. S. Regs., Part II. and the Staff Manual respectively. Title Pages will be prepared in manuscript.

Place	Date	Hour	Summary of Events and Information	Remarks and references to Appendices
STEENWERCK	26.7.16		A.D.M.S orders received this F.A. to take over R.A.P.s 2, 4, 5 & 6 in addition to three now served	a/w
	27.7.16		Handed over Dressing Station ROMARIN to 36th Div. men accommodated there went back to DOUDOU also on the wagon (turn-out) in B.D.s orders & A.D.M.S. orders cancelled except for above mentioned Dressing Stn. in B.D.s orders + A.D.M.S. orders R.A.Po	a/w
	28.7.16		Rearrangement of trenches. PROWSE PT. DEAD HORSE Corner + RIFLE HOUSE now served by us. The R.A.P at O.19.a.77 is taken over by 36th Div. Working party from NIEPPE withdrawn - only 2 men left as guard. Enemy shelled NIEPPE for about 1 hr. 4-5 p.m. two landed near M.D.S. Benn grave but no casualties among our men.	a/w
	29.7.16		Party sent to 140 F.A. for instruction withdrawn.	a/w
	30.7.16		Nothing to report. Fine Summer weather.	a/w
	31.7.16		Weekly conference.	a/w

M Williamson
Major R.A.M.C.
O.C. 136 F. Amb.

41st Div.
Vol 4

Aug. 1916.

CONFIDENTIAL

WAR DIARY

OF

138th FIELD AMBULANCE R.A.M.C.

FROM AUGUST 1st 1916 (VOLUME 4.) To AUGUST 31st 1916

WAR DIARY
or
INTELLIGENCE SUMMARY

(Erase heading not required.)

Army Form C. 2118

Place	Date	Hour	Summary of Events and Information	Remarks and references to Appendices
STEEN WERCK	1.8.16		An officer 139th F.A. attached to A.D.S. for instruction. A/Williamson Major R.A.M.C.	A/W
	2.8.16		Capt. Knight proceeded to A.D.S. under instruction for one week.	A/W
	5.8.16		Operations in L Sector for straightening line to be carried out to-night. Ordered doubling of R.A.P. personnel. Gas alert 8.30 p.m. Wind very slight.	A/W
	6.8.16		Two casualties last night, none in F.A. personnel. Some shelling of NIEPPE.	A/W
	7.8.16		Lieut Shildeton relieved in charge of work parties by Lieut Wilson 139th F.A.	V.R.
	8.8.16		Ambulance Cars at A.D.S. ordered to be parked behind buildings	V.R.
	9.8.16		Capt. Lauder D.S.O. proceeded on 14 days leave of absence. Telephone sent up to A.D.S. to connect ē BDē H.Q.	A/W
	10.8.16		Telephone communication established.	A/W
	11.8.16		Issued orders under instructions from H.Q. for working parties to be withdrawn from work from 9 – 12 hrs.	A/W
	12.8.16		Wrote relieving Capt. Lauder.	A/W
	13.8.16		Received orders re relief of 41st Div? in area at present occupied. Received 122 Duty.	A/W
	14.8.16		Officers under instruction at A.D.S. from 139 F.A. withdrawn.	A/W
			R.W.R. orders re move to La Creche area.	A/W
	15.8.16		One section of no 71 Field Ambulance arrived & started taking over	A/W
	16.8.16		Party 71st F.A. took over A.D.S. and working party & A.D.S. party of 132nd F.A. returned to Headquarters	A/W

WAR DIARY
or
INTELLIGENCE SUMMARY

(Erase heading not required.)

Army Form C. 2118

Place	Date	Hour	Summary of Events and Information	Remarks and references to Appendices
STEENWERCK	17.8.16	8 a.m	Handing over to 71st F.A. completed and 198th F.A. marched to FLETRE area. map 27 N 11 a 4.2. Motor transport handed over except 2 Cars & 2 Cycles. Remained until entrainment.	A/W
FLETRE	18.8.16		Lt YOUNG returned to F.A. from charge of Div¹ Baths.	A/W
"	19.8.16		Lt Young detached on Bath duties in this area.	A/W
"	20.8.16		Capt. LAUDER returned from leave. Motor cycles sent off to 71st F.A.	A/W
"	21.8.16		Lt Wells (?) proceeded as Billeting Officer to PONT REMY.	A/W
"			122 I.B.D. Orders received re entrainment.	
"	22.8.16		Received 122 I.B.D. orders re Change of Div¹ MO's. Report Officer	A/W
"	23.8.16		Reconnaissance of road to station carried out by Lieut. Roche.	A/W
"	24.8.16	8 a.m	Marched to BAILLEUL. Entrained 11.30 – 12.30 p.m. Left 2.28 p.m. Arrived LONGPRÉ. Returned remainder of M.T. Vehicles to 71st F.A.	A/W
"			LES CORPS SAINTS midnight.	
BOUCHON	25.8.16		Detrained + marched at 2.30 a.m to BOUCHON. Bivouaced and moved into Billets. Started training in field work. O.C's F.A. to be responsible for medical arrangements of their B.E. Groups. M.T. Vehicles + personnel arrived from 17th D.S.	A/W
"	26.8.16		Visited 15th Hants. Reg¹. + inspected proposed unfits. Amb. engaged in field exercises.	A/W
"	27.8.16		Lt YOUNG posted to 13th F. Surrey in m/c in relief of Lt OLIVER who reported this F.A.	A/W
"	28.8.16		Visited 18th K.R.R. + 11 R.W.K. re unfits. Carrying wounded, route march + bathing parade under Capt. Lawder.	A/W

WAR DIARY
or
INTELLIGENCE SUMMARY

Army Form C. 2118

(Erase heading not required.)

Place	Date	Hour	Summary of Events and Information	Remarks and references to Appendices
BOUCHON	29.8.16		Medical Field day carried out in conjunction with 129th & 140th F.Aa. Marched out 7.30 a.m. & returned 7 p.m. C section & (seven subalterns of) A & B Section worked independently. Wet day.	a/w
"	30.8.16		A.D.M.S. inspected a batch of unfits for the Base. Very wet day. Lt. R.R. Watts proceeded to 189th Bde R.F.A. in relief of Lieut. MORRISON evacuated sick.	a/w
"	31.8.16		Fine day. Field training proceeded with	

A/Kelliman
Major RAMC.

190/8115

War Diary,
of
138th Field Amb
41st Division

from
1st September to 30th September
1916

(VOLUME V)

Vol 5

COMMITTEE FOR THE
MEDICAL HISTORY OF THE WAR
Date -9 DEC. 1916

WAR DIARY
or
INTELLIGENCE SUMMARY

(Erase heading not required.)

Army Form C. 2118

Place	Date	Hour	Summary of Events and Information	Remarks and references to Appendices
BOUCHON	1.9.16		Training carried on.	Abraham Singh 2/Lt
AILLY LE H CLOCHER AREA	2.9.16		Route march, rattling parade & general training. Transport inspected by Div¹ train.	a/n 2/Lt
	3.9.16		Made reconnaissance for field day on 4th. LIEUT WELLS COLE swore in No 2 N.Z. Stationary.	a/n
	4.9.16		Marched out to medical field day 6.45. Weather very wet, returned to billets 2 p.m. Reconnaissance SM MATHEWS ABC took gun on W.G. transport on to XV Corps Area. near BERNANCOURT. Received orders for Personnel & transport to entrain.	a/n
	5.9.16			a/n
BERNANCOURT AREA map 62D E15a 5.10	6.9.16		Personnel marched with 122 Inf Bde, group at 2.30 am entrained at LONGPRE LE CORPS SAINT at 5 a.m. Detrained at MERICOURT & marched to Camp at E15.A 5.10 on map 62D arriving there 2.30 p.m. Transport arrived about 10 p.m.	a/n
	7.9.16		Reinforcements 5 Ptes arrived.	
	8.9.16	8 p.m.	Made a reconnaissance of the arrangements of 63rd Div. an to Evacuation from DELVILLE WOOD Sector. Corps M.D.S. for lying down cases at BECORDEL. Div¹ Collecting Sta for walking cases and Div Dressing station at Quarry Sheet 57C. also there. Head quarters R.F.A. (advanced) at GREEN DUMP S.16.C 84. + R.A.P. (at shaft 12 b F 6 a 9.2) (evacs leaves and 6 40 8 10 thence by motor amb). Forward OP that a post for carrying bearers by hand to Quarry thence by horse amb 6. 40 8 10 thence by motor amb at Chatby Trench walking wounded B3 to Corps M.D.S. for duty there with one tent subdivision left for Corps M.D.S. for duty there CAPT KNIGHT & LIEUT OLIVER	a/n
	9.9.16	7 am	CAPT LAUDER D.S.O., L¹ REARDEN + HUDSON with all Bearer subdivisions left for Div. C.S. to be absorbed into duties + taking over. Made reconnaissance of BERNAFAY WOOD Dressing Stn. Cars can get to X roads at S.W. corner of Wood. Carried to there by hand. Bearers changing post at Shrine S 23 a 77.	a/n

WAR DIARY
or
INTELLIGENCE SUMMARY

Army Form C. 2118

Place	Date	Hour	Summary of Events and Information	Remarks and references to Appendices
Sheet 62D 7.6.a.20	10.9.16		Head Qr of 7.A. arrived here to be ready to take over div. dressing stn from 1/1 6 F.A. with 2 tent subdivisions. Remainder of transport & qm. left at BECORDEL.	AW
	11.9.16		Taking over of Qmany complicated by arrival of N.Zealand Division also with orders to take over, however I received orders to take over from the N.Zealanders. I have also a party still at Bernafay wood sharing a dug out with the 55-Div. (1/1 Wessex F.A.) as much of an evacuation is by that route. E N E from MAMETZ from 1/2 Wessex F. amb. on Div. Dressing Sn ½ m. ENE from MAMETZ. Took over Div. Dressing Stn ½ m.	AW
	12.9.16		Visited RAPs on R1. 4 left flank of our area. On a capacious dugout with not much protection on had occupied by 23 Middly Regt. near SHRINE and then went to Green DUMP & CARLTON trench where 90% had gone in with N.Z. Rifle Bn. & found RAP at a point about 100 yds E of junction with communication trench. Arranged with ADMS 14th Divn who are on on Rt to share BERNAFAY W'd RAP and also Div. Coll. station here. N.Z. amb., vacated Qmany I started to have the place put in some sort of sanitary condition.	AW O
	13.9.16		Withdrew party from BERNAFAY WOOD aid post. On account of the traffic control regulations it was clear that F 6 a 2 was impracticable as a RCS. Reconnaissance of MONTAUBAN-CARNOY ROAD made &	

WAR DIARY or INTELLIGENCE SUMMARY

Army Form C. 2118

Place	Date	Hour	Summary of Events and Information	Remarks and references to Appendices
	13 9/6		a Stone Quarry in MONTAUBAN village where bearer ambce. from Quarry could be emptied into motor ambce. by which wounded could be taken to BEAURDEL direct. Notification arrived that 8 new Corps Collecting Station would be opened at A.3.a.38 in field ambce. of the 14th Division. Evacuation from BERNAFAY WOOD to there by horse ambce., there by motor ambce. from Quarry to there by horse ambce. return to Quarry by track through to MAMETZ – MONTAUBAN Road. Arranged with O.C. Collecting Stn that D would close at 6 a.m. & he would open. Evacuation to this point ceased & all cars directed to A.3.a.38. Capt. Hannam & Lieut Lacey v/c at Quarry A.D.S.	A.3.a.38 A.3.a.38
F.6.a.20	14 9/6			

WAR DIARY
or
INTELLIGENCE SUMMARY

(Erase heading not required.)

Army Form C. 2118

Place	Date	Hour	Summary of Events and Information	Remarks and references to Appendices
76.a.20	14.9.16		Capt Rainey, Capt Vickers, to REARDEN, HUDSON & THOMAS proceeded to Quarry A.D.S. with one test subdivision. Capt LAUDER with Capt CORKHILL & Bearer div. 139th F.A. + one bearer subdivision 138 F.A. proceeded to SHRINE S.23.a.88. Major WILMOT & Capt HOGG + Bearer div. 140th F.A. + one bearer subdivision 138 F.A. proceeded to GREEN DUMP S.16.c.94.	✓
			M.O. I/c 18 K.R.R. requested bearers to accompany him on the Rgt. was to move from CARLTON TRENCH to TEA TRENCH through the night. 8 Bearers were sent. Similarly M.O. I/c 15th HANTS. moved his with his Regt. from FRENCH LANE to PEACH TRENCH at 1 a.m.	✓

Army Form C. 2118

WAR DIARY
or
INTELLIGENCE SUMMARY
(Erase heading not required.)

Place	Date	Hour	Summary of Events and Information	Remarks and references to Appendices
15.9.16	15/9/16		The 41st Div'n formed centre of attacking force for the capture of FLERS with N.Z. Div on left & 14th Div'n on right.	A/W
			Arrangements for evacuation. R.A.Ps. as follows 18 K.R.R. TEA TRENCH 13 Hants PEACH TRENCH carriage by hand to Quarry A.D.S. then Bearer aid Posts at GREEN DUMP & SHRINE	
			Later it was found possible to use Motor Ambs. for this carry. From there G.D.S. at first only Horse Ambs. could be used but later it was possible to use Motor Ambs to C. Collecting Station on the MONTAUBAN - CARNOY road from which casualties were taken to C.C.S. for walking wounded at M.D.S. both of which were at BECORDEL.	
			It was found impossible after the casualties began to come in quickly to keep even nominal rolls with accuracy. In names of 1170 were taken but it is certain that many were passed through on returning empty wagons of all sorts without this being done. There was in fact a rush of wounded	

WAR DIARY
or
INTELLIGENCE SUMMARY
(Erase heading not required.)

Army Form C. 2118

Place	Date	Hour	Summary of Events and Information	Remarks and references to Appendices
Septh	15/16		Lasting throughout the day & night. It was about 6 a.m. on 16th before the last car was got off, but evacuation was proceeding smoothly by midnight. In the course of the afternoon there was an accumulation of about 200 stretcher cases awaiting space, but these were cleared & hut was reduced to a very small number by 9 p.m.	O/W
		8 a.m.	O.C. Bearers R. Sector opened a further aid post in front of DELVILLE WOOD & reported wounded by Ford cars possible. It was not until midday that cars arrived to him there as they were used up on the road — RAPs at FLERS	
		12 noon	A further aid post opened at Bluff S.6.d.22. (later N.21.d.36. and S.6.b.99) By this time the advance had crossed BULLS ROAD.	
			Lieut HUDSON sent to 15th HANTS & Lieut REARDEN to Middlesex Regt. to replace casualties in their MOs	

WAR DIARY / INTELLIGENCE SUMMARY

Army Form C. 2118

Place	Date	Hour	Summary of Events and Information	Remarks and references to Appendices
	16/10		Relief of bearers arranged for. 170 men of R.W.Kents, Bearer Subdivs N.Z.F.A., Bearer Subdiv. from 21st Bn. arrived + were posted. O'Brien + 2 officers + 2 bearer Subdivs, N.Z.F.A. between R.O.Po. + bluff Sqd.22. 21st Bn. to work between them + shrine. Capt. ROWBOTHAM to relieve MAJOR WILMOT at GREEN DUMP with 50 men of 1st Bn. About 5 p.m. learned that N.Z. station had been withdrawn without my knowledge + was informed that they were forming an A.D.S. of their own forward of LONGEVAL. Late in evening R.W.Kents were also withdrawn.	M/W
		8pm	Runners received of large numbers of wounded in shed about FLERS (G.00) partially rested bearers BROWN + GREEN TRENCHES. All parties not taken to SHRINE + sent + also in spared from Green Dump were taken to BROWN. could be spared from Green Dump — about 40 + bought M in parties under Lieut ROCHE + LIEUT POOLE (21st Bn) + Serjt. BROWN. They reported to 6th Bde H.Q. + were directed to wounded to be in vicinity of bluff Sqd.22. them in. LIEUT POOLE during FLERS — LIEUT ROCHE + Serjt. BROWN — BROWN + GREEN TRENCHES. motor convoy arrived at SHRINE about midnight but there were very few cases to bring. Received information that Pte Calthoft + Dalton were killed this morning on a shell between LONGEVAL + FLERS. Impossible for me to arrange	M/W

WAR DIARY
or
INTELLIGENCE SUMMARY
(Erase heading not required.)

Army Form C. 2118

Instructions regarding War Diaries and Intelligence Summaries are contained in F. S. Regs., Part II. and the Staff Manual respectively. Title Pages will be prepared in manuscript.

Place	Date	Hour	Summary of Events and Information	Remarks and references to Appendices
Sheet 62 D E 15 a.	17.9.16		About noon word was received that we would be relieved by the D. 5-8th Divs and to expect a party to arrive forthwith. It was not however till late in the evening that a small party of Officers arrived at the Quarry. The transport of personnel arrived about midnight. I took the Officers round up to the SHRINE from which two Officers with a party of the bearers went forward to relieve our bearers & and in doing were wounded viz in the neighbourhood of FLERS, Capts LAUDER & CORKHILL. The went as guides and at 6 a.m. the relief was reported clear and at 5. a.m. the Officers reporting the relief to be complete with 5.6. Div.2	M/W
	18.9.16		T.O. moved Office & motor ambulance cars Left 4 motor amb. cars with 5.6. Div. Picked up transport at Fere & marched via dry weather tracks to PRICOURT after which was allowed to use the road via MEAULT. Pouring rain all the time. Arrived in Camp about 2 p.m. drew shelters, put up hospital tents.	M/W
	19.9.16		Checked men & equipment & started to refit. Weather cold, wet, windy. Camp a quagmire. Prepared report on action. ADMS visited camp.	
	20.9.16		Completed report on action. Men bathed at Corps Baths.	

Army Form C. 2118

WAR DIARY
or
INTELLIGENCE SUMMARY

(Erase heading not required.)

Instructions regarding War Diaries and Intelligence Summaries are contained in F.S. Regs., Part II. and the Staff Manual respectively. Title Pages will be prepared in manuscript.

Place	Date	Hour	Summary of Events and Information	Remarks and references to Appendices
BUIRE D23c71	22/9/16	noon	Received a wire yesterday to take over Y Corps Rest Stn here. Arrived 6 pm & finished taking over at 6 a.m. to-day. Received a wire yesterday about 3 p.m. A.D.M.S. evacuated sick proceeded H.Q. 7.30 & arranged to take over duties from to-day. Capt. H.W. HODGSON arrived & posted to this 9. Amb. Arranged for replenishment of med. & surg. equipment for 122 Infy. Bde. Supplies rec'd 2/0 140 F.A. 5 p.m.	A/W
	23/9/16	noon	Proceeding with straightening out of Y corps Rest Stn.	A/W
	24/9/16	6pm	Inclus both home Rest Stn, the night 25th & 26th being walking	A/w
	25/9/16		Admitted 360 cases during the night 25th & 26 wounded.	A/w
	26/9/16		Col. RATTRAY took over duties of A.D.M.S. 41st Div. Capt. J. LOUDON arrived & was taken on the strength.	A/L
	27/9/16		D.M.S. XV Corps Surg. Genl. O'KEEFE visited Rest Stn. weather very fine since 22nd but very showery to-day.	M/w
	28/9/16		Lt REARDEN struck off strength to permanent charge of 23rd Middlesex Regt. Received information that CRS accommodation is to be increased to 1200.	A/w
	30/9/16		No further event of importance	

A. Mc...
Brig... Rgnr.

War Diary.

138th Field Amb

October 1916

41st Divn

WAR DIARY or INTELLIGENCE SUMMARY

Army Form C. 2118
Vol VI SHEET 1

Place	Date	Hour	Summary of Events and Information	Remarks and references to Appendices
S 11 C9H	11.10.16	7am	at 1.30pm hrs from A.D.M.S. that 3th Bde would take over from one & the F.A. to go on relief to 124 Infy BDE. Camp at 7 B.C. During the afternoon the vicinity of the Green Dump was shelled intermittently. One man of the 9.A. was slightly wounded. Any other casualties in neighbouring units & fires of on horses were hit. One of these had to be destroyed. Operation order received 7pm. — Relief to be complete by 8 a.m.	A/R
7 8 C	12.10.16	10 a.m.	Marched out of Green Dump at 8 a.m. Yesterday to marched Dump at X 29 d 42 + annexed Ba. then marched on to 7 8 C. + reported X 29 d 42 + 124 Infy Bde. LIEUT HUDSON reported at X 29 d 42 on discharge from Corps Rest Stn. He was i/c braves on the afternoon @ 10.10.16 on discharge from Corps Rest Stn. He was i/c braves the nyt wr by 30th 2nd 10.10.16 Then retired at McCORMACK'S POINT during F. Amb. braves Sent LIEUTS ROCHE + CONNOLLY to C.C.S. for Walking Wounded at 11pm with 2 N.C.O.s. clothing &c. at 9am. LIEUT PICKIN reported his Inspected Gas Helmets, posted to the F. Amb. at 12 NOON. arrived	A/R
BOIRRE D23 C71	13.10.16	2pm	Moved from Camp with 124 Infy Bde by route march to BOIRRE. Accommodated at Corps Rest Station withdrawn motor ambs. from C.O.S. for W.W. CAPT BINNEY/ proceeded on 14 days contract leave.	

Army Form C. 2118

WAR DIARY
or
INTELLIGENCE SUMMARY
(Erase heading not required.)

Instructions regarding War Diaries and Intelligence Summaries are contained in F. S. Regs., Part II. and the Staff Manual respectively. Title Pages will be prepared in manuscript.

Place	Date	Hour	Summary of Events and Information	Remarks and references to Appendices
BOIRRE ⑂23 c71	14.10.16	6 a.m.	LIEUT HUDSON proceeded with 124th Infy Bde Staff as Billetting Officer	
	15.10.16		Recalled Capt KNIGHT & 2/Lieut OLIVER with tent section from 4 Corps MDS BECORDEL. LIEUTS ROCHE & CONNOLLY returned from CCS. Capt. KNIGHT with Lieut ROCHE & Lt. 2/m m	
	16.10.16		Transport marched 10.15 a.m. under Capt. KNIGHT DODDS for destination FRESNE TILLALOY by road Received I.O.O.'s	
	17.10.16			
	17.10.16		Marched to RIBEMONT & entrained 1.30 pm. Ambulance Convoy by road under Lt. CONNOLLY. Lieut PICKIN detained as billeting Officer at AMIENS	
	18.10.16		Arrived 5.10 a.m OISEMONT – marched to FRESNE TILLALOY	
	19.10.16		Continued in FRESNE-TILLALOY – O.O's received 10.30 p.m	
	20.10.16		Ambulance Convoy under Capt KNIGHT AE proceeded to CAESTRE. Field Ambulance marched to PONT REMY – entrained 4.10 pm.	
	21.10.16		Arrived CODERSWELDE 4.0 am. Marched to billets in CAESTRE. Lieut HUDSON P. posted in permanent medical charge of 15th Hants	
	23.10.16	2 pm	Continued in CAESTRE billets until 12 noon – relieved O.O's and advance party proceeded to take over D.R.S. WIPPENHOEK from the 13th Australian Field Ambulance Rest of Field Ambulance marched off at 1 pm.	
	24.10.16	6.00 am	Took over D.R.S. WIPPENHOEK Lieut OLIVER & 24 other ranks took over Scabies Hospital, BOESCHÉPE (R 9 c 10 zero). Lieut CONNOLLY & 12 other ranks took over Detention Hospital, STEENVORDE (Q 1 B 2 3.)	

1875 Wt. W593/826 1,000,000 4/15 I.P.C. & A. A.D.S.S./Forms/C. 2118.

Army Form C. 2118

WAR DIARY
or
INTELLIGENCE SUMMARY
(Erase heading not required.)

Instructions regarding War Diaries and Intelligence Summaries are contained in F. S. Regs., Part II. and the Staff Manual respectively. Title Pages will be prepared in manuscript.

3

Place	Date	Hour	Summary of Events and Information	Remarks and references to Appendices
WIPPENHOECK	24/10/16		Water Wardens were also posted as under :- 2 other ranks at L 3 2. & 6.4. 2 other ranks at R 2. a 3.3.	
	25/10/16		Received wire to detail 2 men as Water Wardens at E.Y. BECQUE (P12 a 5.7) reported compliance. Later- S.301 received - Lieut CONNOLLY + 12 other ranks to be relieved from Detention Hospital, STEENVOORDE - also the 2 Water Wardens at P12 a 5.7 - by 139th Field Ambulance	
	26.10.16		Relief completed 12 noon - arrived A.D.M.S of arrival at D.R.S. of the relieved parties	
	27.10.16		Lieut CONNOLLY detailed to report to O.C. 11th Royal West Surreys as M.O. in temporary relief of Lieut G.P. WHITE.	
	28.10.16		D.D.M.S. X Corps inspected D.R.S.	
	29.10.16		Lieut + Q.M. DODDS proceeded on 10 days leave	
			Capt BINNEY reported his arrival from leave - 12 noon	
	31.10.16		Capt KNIGHT, A.E. reported to Sanitary Section as temporary O.C. in relief of Capt VICKERS	
	1.11.16		Scabies Hospital, BOESCHEPE transferred to School House in accordance with A.D.M.S. instructions	

CONFIDENTIAL. Vol 7

WAR DIARY

OF

138th FIELD AMBULANCE.

FROM:- NOVEMBER 1ST 1916. (VOLUME VII.) TO:- NOVEMBER 30TH 1916.

COMMITTEE FOR THE
MEDICAL HISTORY OF THE WAR
Date   13 MAR. 1917

WAR DIARY or INTELLIGENCE SUMMARY

Army Form C. 2118

138th Field Ambulance Vol VII Page 1

Place	Date	Hour	Summary of Events and Information	Remarks and references to Appendices
WIPPENHOECK	2/11/16		G.O.C. inspected the camp.	
	5/11/16		attended conference at A.D.M.S.	
	6/11/16		Lieut. PICKIN, E.H. RAMC, under instructions from A.D.M.S. reported for duty as temporary M.O. i/c C.R.E. in relief of LIEUT. MULLOY, RAMC granted 14 days leave.	
	9/11/16		Lieut. CONNOLLY, RAMC, on being relieved by LIEUT. G.P. WHITE, RAMC, reported as temporary M.O. i/c C.R.E. 41st Division in relief of LIEUT. E.H. PICKIN, RAMC. LIEUT. E.H. PICKIN, RAMC has now reported for duty to A.D.M.S. 25th Division. CAPT. KNIGHT, A.E. although not struck off the strength of this unit, will take over entire supervision of sanitary arrangements for this area. 63805 Pte Brookes H. awarded Military Cross	
	12/11/16		38368 Sgt Major Ratcliffe E. granted 10 days leave from 12/11/16 to 21/11/16 inclusive	
	13/11/16		Capt. C.N. BINNEY, RAMC relieved LIEUT. L.W. OLIVER, RAMC at Leabies Hospital, BOESCHÈPE	
	14/11/16		LIEUT L.V. OLIVER, RAMC reported to D.R.S.	
	15/11/16		Capt. F.C. DREW, RAMC. posted to this Unit for duty	
	16/11/16		1 Staff Sergt, 1 Sgt & 29 men reported for duty to O.C. 140th Field ambulance Others 1 for duty. P/JM Matthews E (A.S.C. attached) granted 10 days leave from 16/11/16 to 25/11/16 inclusive	

WAR DIARY
or
INTELLIGENCE SUMMARY

Army Form C. 2118

138th Field Ambulance Vol. VII Pages 11

Place	Date	Hour	Summary of Events and Information	Remarks and references to Appendices
NIPPEN HOECK	19/11/16	—	Lt Col. A.J. WILLIAMSON, R.A.M.C. relinquishes his temporary rank as LIEUT COLONEL & reverts to the permanent rank of Major upon ceasing to hold appointment as O.C. 138th Field Ambulance, R.A.M.C. from the 28th ult. CAPT. J LA F. LAUDER, D.S.O. R.A.M.C. awarded Military Cross. Attended conference at A.D.M.S.	
	18/11/16		Capt. J LA F. LAUDER, D.S.O. M.C. R.A.M.C. to be temporary O.C. pending permanent appointment from the 28th ult. N.C.O's & 6 other ranks reported to O.C. Ladies Hospital BOESCHEPE to take over temporarily, the Baths.	
	20/11/16		LIEUT. L.W. OLIVER, R.A.M.C. granted 10 days leave from the 18/11/16 to 29/11/16 inclusive. Capt. F.C. DREW, R.A.M.C. relieved LIEUT WILLIAMSON, R.A.M.C. as M.O. i/c 32nd Royal Fusiliers during latters absence on leave.	
	21/11/16		Capt. W.R. GARDNER, R.A.M.C. (S.R.) reported his arrival & took over command of this unit.	
	23/11/16		Lieut D.I. CONNOLLY, R.A.M.C. being relieved by LIEUT. MULLOY, R.A.M.C. M.O. i/c 11th C.R.E. reported his arrival at D.R.S.	
	24/11/16		Lt. Major E. RATCLIFFE reported his arrival back from leave.	

W.S.

WAR DIARY
or
INTELLIGENCE SUMMARY

(Erase heading not required.)

Army Form C. 2118

138th Field Ambulance
Vol. VIII
Page 111

Place	Date	Hour	Summary of Events and Information	Remarks and references to Appendices
WIPPENHOEK	26/11/16		General S.T.B. LAWFORD, C.B. inspected the camp.	
	27/11/16		Capt. C.N. BINNEY posted as temporary M.O. i/c 18th Kings Royal Rifles in relief of Lieut A.P. HART, R.A.M.C. granted 10 days leave. Capt. J. LOUDON, R.A.M.C. detailed to take over charge of Rabies Hospital, BOESCHEPE during the absence of Capt C.N. BINNEY, R.A.M.C. Working party of 1 Sergt & 30 men detailed to relieve the party at DICKEBUSCH. Sgt. Major E. MATTHEWS reported his arrival back from leave.	
	28/11/16		LIEUT L.W. OLIVER, R.A.M.C. reported his arrival back from leave. 1 Sgt & 2 men now detailed to keep open the SCABIES HOSPITAL, BOESCHEPE the remainder reporting at D.R.S. for duty	
	30/11/16		LIEUT L.W. OLIVER R.A.M.C. detailed to relieve Capt SHEFFIELD R.A.M.C. as M.O. i/c 1st Divisional Train, A.S.C. the latter having been granted 14 days contact leave.	

R MacGardner (S.R.)
Capt RAMC 138th Field Ambulance
O.C. No 138
30th

140/1943

Vol 8

COMMITTEE FOR THE
MEDICAL HISTORY OF THE WAR
Date 13 MAR. 1917

CONFIDENTIAL

War Diary

OF

138th Field Ambulance RAMC

From 1st December 1916 To December 31st 1916.

(Volume VIII.)

WAR DIARY

Army Form C. 2118

Instructions regarding War Diaries and Intelligence Summaries are contained in F.S. Regs., Part II. and the Staff Manual respectively. Title Pages will be prepared in manuscript.

INTELLIGENCE SUMMARY 138th Field Ambulance.
(Erase heading not required.)

Vol. VIII   Page I

Place	Date	Hour	Summary of Events and Information	Remarks and references to Appendices
WIPPENHOEK	1/10/16		Weather — cold, misty. Attended conference at A.D.M.S. at 11 am re elaborate instructions re disposal of a certain number of the personnel of this unit in the event of heavy fighting. No [?] in the W.R.S. at 12 noon today. 41st Draw 171 O.Rs. Dn 11 Total 182 During the past 24 hours 24 have been returned to duty.	S.P.R.9
"	2/9/16		Weather — cold, mist. Seven reinforcements arrived and were taken on the strength accordingly. 18 O.R. returned to duty today	W.R.9
"	3/10/16		Frosty weather. Lieut. W.J. CONNOLLY R.A.M.C. (T.C.) reported to D.C. 15th Hants. in relief of Captain TODD R.A.M.C who is over. Captain F.C. DREW R.A.M.C (T.C.) rejoined the unit on relief by Lieut. WILLIAMSON R.A.M.C returned from leave. 3/3 O.R. returned to duty today.	W.R.9
"	4/10/16		Cool as showery — was 5 cases. All the horse transport inspected by D.C. 41st Divisional Train at 9.30 am. Major Gen Lawford C.B. Commanding 41st Division made a tour of inspection The Divisional Rest Station. Captain F.C. DREW R.A.M.C (T.C.) attended a conference at A.D.M.S at 3 pm. Fourteen O.Rs. ranks returned to duty today.	W.R.9

WAR DIARY
or
INTELLIGENCE SUMMARY

(Erase heading not required.)

138ᵗʰ Field Ambulance

Vol VIII   Page 11

Army Form C. 2118

Place	Date	Hour	Summary of Events and Information	Remarks and references to Appendices
WIPPENHOEK	5/10/16		Weather showery, milder. Bras O/S.	WRG
	6/10/16		Shuty. Three other ranks returned to duty today. Weather cold, wind. A.D.M.S. H/Qtrs Wks. inspected all ranks at 2.30pm. Patients hospital surroundings. 16 O.R's returned to duty today.	WRG
"	7/10/16		Inv. Medy. Board held at 9.30 by A.D.M.S. H/Qtrs Wks. to examine those men recommended for P.B.	WRG
	8/10/16		Weather — advanced. 2 reinforcements arrived from the Base, and were collected from Other Ambulance now up to War Estabt.	WRG
	9/xiii/16		39 other ranks returned to duty today. DDMS X Corps inspects the 10th Post Station today. Captain C.N. BINNEY R.A.M.C. (T.C.) rejoined from 21st K.R.R.C.	WRG
	10/10/16		47 other ranks returned to duty today. Showery. 14 O/R's returned to duty today.	WRG
	11/10/16		Bright & clear. 17 other ranks returned to duty. Sgt MANN R.A.M.C. arrived from No XII advanced Depot of Medical Stores. Stores taken on Ambce strength.	WRG

WAR DIARY
or
INTELLIGENCE SUMMARY

Army Form C. 2118

136th Field Ambulance
Vol. VIII Page 111

Place	Date	Hour	Summary of Events and Information	Remarks and references to Appendices
WIPPEN HOEK	12/10/16	—	Weather cats showery. Carried being held twice weekly for the patients of Divisional Rest Station. Shaken stretchers returned to clng today.	WDB
	13/10/16		Weather fine. 16 other ranks returned to clng today.	WDB
	14/10/16		Weather fine. Returned breast hearths A.D.M.S met Chi on TV & PB man Brent. From the March returns lately today.	WDB
			Attended conference at A.D.M.S and also well as many orderlies. Conference at A.D.M.S, and also late of Gradient Phenomena on the SOMME. Just for return today Summary	WDB
	15/10/16			
	16/10/16		Weather important. Lt OLIVER R.A.M.C. reports from temporary duty weather fine though, Jenkin other ranks returned to duty today with the H1st Divisional train.	WDB
	17/10/16			WDB
	18/10/16		Weather — cols wdny. Lt D CONNOLLY R.A.M.C. detailed to report to O.C 11th R.W. KENTS for temporary duty. Marks number parts an infected bullets at W.D.R.	WDB
			From the rends returns today.	
			CAPTAIN J. LOUDON R.A.M.C detailed for medical examining duties with X. Corps. Cavalry Regiment tomorrow.	WDB

1875 Wt. W593/826 1,000,000 1/15 T R.C. & A. A.D.S.S./Forms/C. 2118.

WAR DIARY
or
INTELLIGENCE SUMMARY

Army Form C. 2118

138th Field Ambulance Volume VIII Page IV

(Erase heading not required.)

Place	Date	Hour	Summary of Events and Information	Remarks and references to Appendices
WIPPENHOEK	19/10/16	—	Weather cold & showery. Escort for the patient at 5.30 pm G.D.C's. Show bus transport. Capt [?] Rane enrolls 4 sergeant recruits for letter Cycle in accordance with A.O. M.G's instructions.	1/2g
	25/10/16		The ranks return to duty today. Captain L.S. ROCHE RAMC proceeds to England — five & eight days contract leave of absence to 3/10/16	6/2g
	26/10/16		The ranks returned to duty today	6/2g
	27/10/16		The ranks returned to duty today	7/2g
	28/10/16		The ranks returned to duty today	7/2g
	29/10/16		The ranks returned to duty today	7/2g
	30/10/16		The ranks returned to duty today	
	31/10/16		The ranks returned to duty today. Lost Sunday. 27 of the ranks returned to duty today. Capt Sunday with Chaim Dravia. RMS. Team Army Bought Sunday entertains the patients of personnel. A meeting in the camp to usher the bright new year also G.D.C of the Rev. Dastry known a bright new year. Escort for patients Hist. Div. also AAMC Hist Div. 6.30 pm to 8.30 pm.	4/2g
	30/10/16		Attachment form WRaudenbur RAMC grants leave of absence from 27/10/16 Capt Corner RAMC C.S. to 6/11/17 Army div.	6/2g

WAR DIARY or INTELLIGENCE SUMMARY

138th Field Ambulance   Army Form C. 2118
Volume VIII Page V

Place	Date	Hour	Summary of Events and Information	Remarks and references to Appendices
Poperinghe	27.12.16		Lt Col W. R. A. Gardner proceeded to England on ordinary leave of absence. Weather bright & sharp. Evening closes with rain. A concert for patients given by Divisional Concert Party 5 pm – 7 pm. For personnel from 7.80 pm – 9 pm by same. Panos of Gas Helmets, etc.	9A8
	28.12.16		A.D.M.S. holds his usual weekly inspection of T.U. & P.B. with prospector of Transport motor ambulance satisfactory. Weather threatening & stormy.	9E8
	29.12.16		Work party of Personnel attended A.D.M.S. conference.	9C3
	30.12.16		The S.O.T.'s Band gave a performance from 5.30 pm – 7.30 pm.	9.D8
	31.12.16		The Exam in D.R.S at 12 noon. Today 100 visitors attended - 15 - Total 115. Weather cloudy but held. Service for patients held at 3 pm (Presbyterian)	

J. C. Drew
Capt R.A.M.O

140/1943. Vol 9

CONFIDENTIAL.

WAR DIARY

OF

138TH FIELD AMBULANCE R.A.M.C.

FROM JAN. 1ST 1917. TO JAN 31ST 1917.

(VOLUME 9.)

COMMITTEE FOR THE
MEDICAL HISTORY OF THE WAR
Date   13 MAR. 1917

WAR DIARY
or
INTELLIGENCE SUMMARY

Army Form C. 2118

138th Field Ambulance Pass I 1st I 1917

Place	Date	Hour	Summary of Events and Information	Remarks and references to Appendices
Morphenhoek	1.1.17		Lt. Connolly reported at D.R.S. on night of 31.12.16. having been relieved by M.O. i/c charge of 11/12 Royal West Kent relieved from ham - Wrote the firm & Brig.	J.L.B
			A word of best wishes for the New Year received from the Divisional Commander.	
	2.1.17		Inspection of A coy for scabies &c. No case found in the Section. Capt W.H. Chesney M.C. R.A.M.C. reported at H.Q. Divisional Rest Station. a - hole to be duly located tonight a mules - No. of patients to hospital 12 noon. M.G. Dir. 1 2.3 Other 20 Total 1+3-	J.L.B
	3.1.17		The transport was inspected by me at 8 P.M. all vehicles were clean & in good order, horses all in good condition & well - Inspection of tin helmets the field Also stretchers inspection of B sections no defects found in the section. No patients 43 Div. in D.R.S. at 12 noon 15-8.	J.L.B
	4.1.17		Received Maj. Hilston A.D.M.S. Capt. Ancham reports his return from leave. Inspection of C Section all clean -	J.L.B

WAR DIARY or INTELLIGENCE SUMMARY

Army Form C. 2118

138th Field Ambulance Vol. I 1917

Place	Date	Hour	Summary of Events and Information	Remarks and references to Appendices
Coppernolbook	5.1.17		Weather bright + warm. Court prov. by ff. proceeded thing events at 6. P.M. until 7 P.M.	
			Conference of C.O.s of Fld. Ambulances with D.D.M.S. office of A.D.M.S. - Rear 500.87	J.C.D
	6.1.17		Visited with Lt. Col. Cockburn A.D.S of 140 Field Ambulance. A.D.S at Vlebelton + also H.Q.S at Brielenhoek. Together with the S. Officers, attended lecture at 140 F.A. given by Capt. Moore on means of dealing with Rats. Lunched with men at 41 S.R.S. by party from 6 London Field Ambulance. Sgt. Mackintosh + Pt. Carney proceed to Hazebrouck for a course of Instruction in Scabies. To report at Northaulins C.C.S. on 7.1.17. Lt. Col. W. Ross Gordon reports removal after ordinary leave to England.	J.C.D
	7.1.17		Capt. Moore of 138 F.A. + party of 1 N.C.O as other ranks proceeds to take over from 140 F.A. at A.D.S. Mickelbush + R.A.P. Moortseele + Moorneezele + at A.D.S (stretcher posts 1) at Bedford House. Lt. Hale proceeds to Sanitary School at Bochepe for course of Instruction. Sanitary fatigue men at Bochepe returned to party from 140 F.A. Also water party men at Bochepe sent to 140 F.A. uleconoty bath 140 F.A at Athile Thornhurst.	J.C.D
		8 P.M.		

… Army Form C. 2118

WAR DIARY
INTELLIGENCE SUMMARY

(Erase heading not required.)

138th Field Ambulance
Vol. I
1917

Pages III

Place	Date	Hour	Summary of Events and Information	Remarks and references to Appendices
Wippenhoek	8.1.17		Capt Chaney R.A.M.C. 1 N.C.O. & 9 other Ranks took over billets at Renninghelst at 7.12am. Capt DAVIES R.A.M.C. 140th F.A. moved at 10 a.m. for instruction into trenches. CAPTAIN J. LOUDON R.A.M.C. with 3 N.C.O's and 11 O.R. proceeded to DUDERDOM. M.D.S. and took over from 140th F.A. Lt CONNOLLY R.A.M.C. proceeded to DICKEBUSH A.D.S. Lt OLIVER R.A.M.C. proceeded to Engineers in respect of contracts unsettled at the clearing it accordingly.	W109
	9.1.17		Met O.C. 140th F.A. at RENNING HELST. Captain ROCHE R.A.M.C. proceeded to Renninghelst and took morning sick at 9am. Capt HOGG R.A.M.C. moved at the I.C.R.S. at 10am. from 140th F.A. Captain DREW R.A.M.C. left I.C.R.S. with Westoutre T7 Personnel and equipment & reported same at RENNING HELST M.D.S. at 11.30am. Taking completing the move by 11.30am. the day. Under instructions from A.D.M.S. III Corps. I proceeded to DUDERDOM. M.D.S. to meet the Army Commander's inspection of the clearing station. There at 2.30 p.m. A.D.M.S. notified that work had been completed. Officer and 34 O.R. in An.I.O.S. at 12 noon.	W109

WAR DIARY or INTELLIGENCE SUMMARY

Army Form C. 2118

138th Field Ambulance Page IV Month January 1917

Place	Date	Hour	Summary of Events and Information	Remarks and references to Appendices
~~Hoof~~ RENNINGHELST	10.1.17		Capt. LOUDON R.A.M.C. taken over the duties has to now obtained at BEDFORD HOUSE A.D.S. for details.	W28
do	11.1.17		Inspection of Gas helmets among returns. Inspected A.D.S. at DICKEBUSH and R.A.P's at VOORMEZEELE and SPOILBANK.	W28
do	12.1.17		Attended conference at A.D.M.S. received instructions re hospitalization stores etc. Received from A.D.M.S. letter M.787 following him special instructions for the Conveyance of infectious cases at the disposal of R.A.P's Scabies infection convenient	W28
do	13.1.17		Inspected Dickebush A.D.S. & VOORMEZEELE A.D.S. Instructions received from A.D.M.S. today M.853 to withdraw instructions that ambulance received also to our ambulance at LILLE GATE ... YPRES. but to put 2 N.C.O's to await Batts.	W28
do	14.1.17		Car withdrawn from LILLE GATE to DUDERDOM M.D.S. 2 N.C.O's posted to the Divl Baths. Arrangements made to relieve 15 b 30 Can. Scottish has latrines erected at M.D.S. RENNINGHELST.	W28
do	15.1.17		The 2 special trolleys" with the words " FOR WOUNDED ONLY" painted on each side have handed one today, K.M.O. i/c R.A.P. SPOILBANK.	W29

Army Form C. 2118

WAR DIARY
or
INTELLIGENCE SUMMARY

(Erase heading not required.)

Pages V
138th July November January 1917. Vol I

Place	Date	Hour	Summary of Events and Information	Remarks and references to Appendices
RENNINGHELST	16.1.17		4 Officers and 57 O.R. to M.10.S Renninghelst at 12 noon. Report forwarded to ADMS that bags were on ground floor had been out ready for partition. Groundsheets from 37th & 145th Divisions.	WD8
	17.1.17		A.F.W.M.S. No. 619 received detailing one M/T Ambulance for duty at BEDFORD HOUSE ADS from about all dawn	WD8
	18.1.17		Two cars sketches at DICKEBUSCH ADS in a temporary measure in accordance with A.D.M.S. No. S 354	WD8
	19.1.17		VOORMEZEELE R.A.P. and SPOILBANK R.A.P. relieved today. Arrangements made for reinforcing Nine R.O's to deal with the casualties. Lieut CONOLLY R.A.M.C. granted 10 days leave of absence to England.	WD8
	20.1.17		Only 12 casualties passed through the field Ambulance of which 7 were to attending to their wants. Lt General LAWSON C.B. asst ADMS inspector the M. 10 today. Inspector. OUDERDOM ADS BEDFORD HOUSE ADS	WD8
	21.1.17			WD8
	22.1.17		shelters VOORMEZEELE R.A.P. and SPOILBANK R.A.P. and howitzer in the special hollup has been taken away. The evening however additional signs for walking wounded, put up in SCOTCH WOOD CONVENT LANE and ECLUSE TRENCH. The four Kempos at BEDFORD HOUSE ADS relieved & reports.	WD8

WAR DIARY
or
INTELLIGENCE SUMMARY (Erase heading not required.)

Army Form C. 2118

Page vi
138th Field Ambulance Vol I January 1917

Place	Date	Hour	Summary of Events and Information	Remarks and references to Appendices
BRANDHOEK	23.1.17		Captain J L LAUDER RAMC reported his arrival for duty from England, was taken in Mishaght's accurately	WD9
	24.1.17		Pte GLADWELL to England for a commission.	WD9
	25.1.17		Gas helmets, box Respirators etc. inspected. Gas alert ordered at 9 pm	WD9
	26.1.17		Officers conference at A.D.M.S. Death inspection carried out	WD9
	27.1.17		Capt LOUDON RAMC reported to O C 21st KRRC for permanent medical charge. Glycerine supplied to the M.O.S. for distribution to all the Riflemen for the hay Respirators valves. Twelve pack horse Respirator heaters wet Glycerine	WD9
	28.1.17		Additional signs (10) for trenches, wounded erected on ECLUSE LANE, SCOTTISH WOOD the Imphal SPOILBANK RAP VOORMEZEELE RAP and A.D.S. DICKEBUSH. Sign boards with the word "SIDING FOR WOUNDED" erected at the tramway sidings, services by Engineers	WD9
	30.1.17		Officers conference at A.D.M.S. Reeves wheeled Jarrow of additional stores. Capt BINNEY RAMC at the A.D.S.	WD9
	31.1.17		Capt ROCHE RAMC detailed to relieve Capt BINNEY RAMC at the A.D.S.	WD9

W R Gardner, RAMC
Lt Col
O.C. 138th Field Ambulance

140/2042
41st Div

Vol 10

ORDERLY ROOM
No. A.4.12
DATE 26.2.17
138th FIELD AMBULANCE

COMMITTEE FOR THE
MEDICAL HISTORY OF THE WAR
Date   11 MAY.1917

10 February 28th 1917

Confidential

War Diary

of

138th Field Ambulance

(Volume 2.)

from 1st February 1917

WAR DIARY or INTELLIGENCE SUMMARY

Army Form C. 2118

138th Field Ambulance Vol II Page I February 1917

Place	Date	Hour	Summary of Events and Information	Remarks and references to Appendices
RENNINGHELST	1.2.17		Lieut D.J. CONNOLLY RAMC (T.C) rejoined from 10 days ordinary leave to England. Inspected DICKEBUSH A.D.S. and VOORMEZEELE R.A.P. Six Motor Ambulance convoys received from A.D.M.S. 32 D.R's to Hospital belongs to MOTLW. Advances under Instructions from A.D.M.S.	WAR
	2.2.17		Lieut CONNOLLY RAMC reports to O.C. 12th S. Surreys Regt. for 2 days duty in relief of Lt. WILSON RAMC. Captain BINNEY RAMC proceeds to CUNDERDOM on 10.B in relief of Caplan F.C. DREW	WAR
	3.2.17		Caplan F.C. DREW RAMC admitted to Hospital with P.U.O.	WAR
	4.2.17		RAMC operation order No 9 Copy 15 received from A.D.M.S. at 10 am	WAR
	5.2.17		Caplan E.S. ROCHE RAMC detailed for course of Instruction at Army School of Sanitation Ii Armd. Hazelmere. Caplan F.C. DREW RAMC evacuated to No 10 CCS when 77th Strength	WAR
	6.2.17		Instructions received from ADMS 4/2/17th (S. Hov. F 6/2/17) in method of evacuation from BEDFORD HOUSE ADS by day	WAR
	8.2.17		Operation order 85 Copy 13 received appsfrom from 122nd Infantry Brigade, Portion of Battle Stops in the area received from ADMS (S. Hov. 8/2/17) 4 additional bearers posts at SPOILBANK RAP. and 2 additional bearers posts at VOORMEZEELE RAP. 15 wounded evacuated through DICKEBUSH ADS. and 4 wounded through BEDFORD HOUSE ADS. Total 19 wounded.	WAR

WAR DIARY or INTELLIGENCE SUMMARY

Army Form C. 2118

38 N. Field Ambulance Vol II February 1917
Pass II

Place	Date	Hour	Summary of Events and Information	Remarks and references to Appendices
RENNINGHELST	9.2.17		Capt. E P EVANS RAMC reported his arrival from No. 13 General Hospital Boulogne and was taken on the strength accordingly.	MCG
	10.2.17		Additional bearers still retained at SPOILBANK RAP & VOORMEZEELE RAP. Allotted as before at A/DMS.	MCG MCG
	11.2.17		Captain ROCHE RAMC returned from the Course of sanitation and joined bearers withdrawn from the R.A.P.'s	MCG
	12.2.17		Corps. hospital inspected by D.DMS. 8. 9th Corps. Capt. C N BINNEY RAMC detailed to attend Course of sanitation at HAZEBROUCK. Capt. ROCHE RAMC proceeded to ADMS on O/C.	MCG
	13.2.17 to 16.2.17		Nothing of note took place	MCG
	17.2.17		Capt. BINNEY RAMC returned from Second Army School of Sanitation. Capt. C N BINNEY RAMC returned to O.C. 12th E. Surrey Regt (another M.O.J).	MCG MCG
	19.2.17		Capt. WILSON RAMC reported his arrival for duty, relieving Capt. C N BINNEY.	MCG
	20.2.17		Lieut A.M. CRAWFORD RAMC reports his arrival for duty from No. 1 General Hospital turned in very through recently. Units interchange from M.M.S. The bearers at SPOILBANK RAP were increased to 12. and 2 cars were allotted to report to O/c BEDFORD HOUSE A 10 5. to be at his disposal until drawn. 17 cars from 6th LONDON Regt. were evacuated to C.C.S.	MCG
	21.2.17		Anderdon M. 103 and DICKEBUSH A 108 to VOORMEZEELE RMP	MCG

1875 Wt. W593/826 1,000,000 4/15 J.B.C. & A. A.D.S.S./Forms/C.2118.

WAR DIARY or INTELLIGENCE SUMMARY

Army Form C. 2118

Vol II

138th Field Ambulance   Pages III   February 1917

Place	Date	Hour	Summary of Events and Information	Remarks and references to Appendices
RENNINGHELST	22.2.17		nothing of note	
	23.2.17		G.O. 16. Copy 16 received from 123rd Inf. Bgde. Concerns move by 10th Divn. 8 additional bearers posted to SPOILBANK R.A.P. as no additional motor ambulance to the A.D.S. G.O. 67 Copy 16 received from 123rd Inf. Bgde giving details of parts.	W28
	24.2.17		Lieut. A.M. CRAWFORD R.A.M.C. (T.F.) departed for duty with the 46th Divn. Orders received from A.D.M.S. - S.426 23/2/17 to transfer the M.T. personnel & motor Ambulances to the 2/3rd Home (69th Field Ambulance) - the transfer to be completed on the 25/2/17. Capt. ROCHE R.A.M.C. proceeded to 139th Field Ambulance for 24 hour.	W28
	25.2.17		nothing of note	W28
	26.2.17		A.C.S. counter attacks VOORMEZEELE R.A.P. and SPOILBANK R.A.P. trenches	W28
	27.2.17			
	28.2.17		Health of personnel shows marked improvement from January. No outbreak of infectious diseases occurred in the unit.	W29

M. Rae Gauthier R.A.M.C.
Lt/Col R.A.M.C.
O.C. 138th Field Ambulance
D.C.

140/2042 Vol XI

COMMITTEE FOR THE
MEDICAL HISTORY OF THE WAR
Date 11 MAY 1917

CONFIDENTIAL
WAR DIARY
OF
138th FIELD AMBULANCE
From March 1st To March 31st 1917.
(Volume III)

Mar. 1917

WAR DIARY
or
INTELLIGENCE SUMMARY

Army Form C. 2118

Page I

Vol III 1917

Place	Date	Hour	Summary of Events and Information	Remarks and references to Appendices
RENNINGHELST	1.3.17		~3 Officer 47 OR's 7 H/1 at this in hospital	WD8
	2.3.17		Capt ROCHE RAMC reported to O.C. 189th Brigade R.F.A. for temporary duty	WD8
	4.3.17		Capt E.A. LUMLEY RAMC reports his arrival from the train for duty	WD8
	5.3.17		Inspected ADS DICKEBUSCH HUTS REMEZEELE RAP & OUDERDOM M.W.S.	WD8
	6.3.17		Capt E.P. EVANS RAMC (T.C.) departed to BOULOGNE RAF enroute to 10 KMS	WD8
			Base another inspection necessary from HUMS 41st Div, was about 97% strength	
	7.3.17 to 10.3.17		Nothing of note occurred	WD8
	11.3.17		Inspected 43rd FA workshops Infects Invitation to o.s. trench and Adv. VOORMEZEELE R.A.P. & SPOILBANK R.A.P	WD8
	12.3.17		Nothing of note	WD8
	13.3.17		Lieut D.J. CONNOLLY RAMC debates as M.O. I/c 11th R.W.Kent vice Capt. GANN RAMC admitted suffering from P.U.O.	WD8
	14.3.17		D.O. 93 Copy 13 received from 122nd Infantry Brigade	WD8
			Capt R.T. HERDMAN RAMC reports he moved from No 9 General Hospital for duty. Gas helmets inspected.	
	16.3.17		G.O.C. 41st Div. Inspects the A.D.S DICKEBUSCH Steel helmets inspection Personnel cleanliness	WD8

WAR DIARY or INTELLIGENCE SUMMARY

Army Form C. 2118

Page 11
Vol III
1917

Field Ambulance 1/3

Place	Date	Hour	Summary of Events and Information	Remarks and references to Appendices
RENNINGHELST	17.3.17		Usual work.	WDS
	18.3.17		Selected DICKEBUSCH HUTS & VOORMEZEELE R.A.P. & SPEIBANK R.A.P.	WDS
	19.3.17		Graham Bdr No 10 Coy No 1 recvd from No. A.	WDS
	20.3.17		Instruction received from rear A. to S 449 d 29/3/17 to detail 4 men R.A.M.C. to be present at the BRASSERIE N 6 i.i. about 28 N.N. on the 24/3/17. Nr Conroy sick evacuated to the A.D.S. VIERSTRAAT. No 94 Coy 19 recd from 122 ~ 9 Bde. No 72 " 17 recd from 123rd 9 Bde	WDS
	21.3.17		Usual inspection of transport. Instruction was received. Steel Helmets to be N° S 455/445 d. 22/3/17	WDS
	22.3.17		Instruction received from rear A. H.Q. No S 453 d. 24/3/17 to make the necessary arrangements - received w. S453 d. 24/3/17 to vacate N.M.B. 3rd Infantry future Cay trenches Regt and 9 Coy vacated for Nb. 7th Lahore Batt - respectively. 6 Officers & 52 O.R. in hospital.	WDS
	23.3.17		Weekly conference at the A.D.M.S	WDS

WAR DIARY
INTELLIGENCE SUMMARY

Army Form C. 2118

Pages III
Vol. III
1917

Place	Date	Hour	Summary of Events and Information	Remarks and references to Appendices
RENNINGHELT	26.3.17		Relief by Gunners of 11 R.W. Kent Regt — 9 Battery Chats passes through DICKEBUSH Riff ur. S. by at through. BEDFORD HOUSE Piot. 15 C.E.S. Tns. arrived 1 hour at 11 p.m.	WRS
	26.3.17		B.O. 95 Copy 13 received from 132nd I. Bdgs. Relative to relief	WRS
	27.3.17		Weather Showers	
	28.3.17		Capt. A.P. GRAY — C.V. SPARROW Rifle. Reported arrived	
	29.3.17		11. Set to Rain. Gardiner relieve. Os. presented in hour from 10½ to 10⅜ Capt. Owen acting O.C.	
	30.3.17		Capt Gray Nevis, parts in W.O's, 189 1st R.F.A. Relief of Cnan Ridge Talk. Herris Reported to stay until Capt J.E. Rowledge Relieve. Reported his arrival 4.67/17 received from 2 R.F.A. 4.64	
	31/3/17		at 11 a.m. a/40. Proceeded to DICKEBUSCH & arranged for the billeting of N.O. I. F.A. work party.	

CONFIDENTIAL.

140/2026

You/12

COMMITTEE FOR THE
MEDICAL HISTORY OF THE WAR
Date -6 JUN. 1917

War Diary

OF

138th Field Ambulance.

(Volume IV).

From 1st April 1917.   To 30th April 1917

WAR DIARY or INTELLIGENCE SUMMARY

Army Form C. 2118

Page I

138 Third Australian ___ Nov IV 1917

Place	Date	Hour	Summary of Events and Information	Remarks and references to Appendices
	1.4.17		Capt Sparrow RAME. attached as Asst to DADVS W/2 Bn Train Watering Party it to water Passengers to ADS. River suzen	W2S Nil Nil
	2.4.17		OC(a) A.D.V.S. Enemy very active F.As. DQ(56) Capt.19 1.2 Rt. Rts (Shelling is over Rds.) Cpt (7+) Capt.19 N3 Lep Rts (" ") Capt.17 ((1+t FR3)	Nil Nil Nil
	3.4.17			
	4/4/17 5.4.17		MDVS to Capt & Asst MDVS inspected Camp Supt HDZge horsing & aeroplanes	Nil Nil Nil
	6.4.17		Capt F3 26 R.A.M.C. Repre a punts in Capt in his O.C. 4th Rd Aus Vet Cat Sparrow Capt Cj Sparrow Rejoins reported sick Lt. Vh w.H.l.S.M. Rejoins Reported arrived	
	6.4.17		Su77 ADOVS 475 479 480 486	Nil
	7.4.17		Lt. Weave attached to MDS a donsen	NSY

Page III
Vol. IV 1917

Place	Date	Hour	Summary of Events and Information	Remarks and references to Appendices
	8.4.17		Capt J Foster Palmer. absorbing Comm at 3yr Reliew Nitroling, to with	
	9.4.17		Capt E.B. Hinemann Reeve attached to this Unit & Capt E.F. Worman Reeve posts. (L 491 received)	
	10.4.17		Inspection. Gen Webb new Palmer & Men beheads.	
	11.4.17		Received Parts of the Relieves Finds HQ, at in. Queen of the Belgians in was lives	
			Empre. 2 Dows Menerin an Argen lean Initiative I with	
	12.4.17		Capt Hinemann proceeds to A.D.S. Dieu-creix. Capt Henton proceeds from to Netherwear RES. PK. Weller ordered for this to Mansierce	
	13.4.17		PK Eulerp orbs for Comm in bookmaking at Calais Goes with from Schemes to San Labor Pte Nevices Sydenham.	
	14.4.17		L/cp 10.1 Curry 19 to Lit. Net: rennes	
	15.4.17		S.S. 107+ 508 M.Ranger.	
	16.4.17		W. Hash Davis Relieve Capt Wilson who reports for duty at this Station	

WAR DIARY or INTELLIGENCE SUMMARY

Army Form C. 2118

Pages III of IV

138 Fld Amb la 1917

Place	Date	Hour	Summary of Events and Information	Remarks and references to Appendices
RENNINGHELST	17.4.17		S/Sgt G.Cox HD Reps. received. Capt L. ROEMMELE relieves Capt COMMUNEREGS as O/c a bearers party at VOORMEZEELE.	WD
	18.4.17		S/Sgt H.R.M.S. Cpl Manners R.A.M.C. admitted from A.D.S. Dicker noses station sick. 2/Lt. WEBB takes charge	WD
	19.4.17		S/Sgt of HQ Regs. Training Men trained evacuated to C.C.S. Rame.	WD
	20.4.17		L.Cpl. W. ROSS GARDNER R.A.M.C. rejoins from leave.	WD
	21.4.17		Ephraim Lover No. 12 C/by N17. ATOMS received working party at VOORMEZEELE relieves. Addresses conference with Capt. J. W. LAUDER	WD
	22.4.17		Capt J L. F LAUDER R.A.M.C. a/chg. 10 A.T.OM.S. Fairbank.	WD
	23.4.17		G.O. 102 C/by No 19 received from 132 Inf Bdys. Lieut W.M. LODD's R.A.M.C. rejoins from leave. Capt A.E. KNIGHT R.A.M.C. (attached ATOMS) granted to VOORMEZEELE	WD
	24.4.17		Valhuna. Scout No 513 received from ADMS 9.10 am Capt WOODWARD R.A.M.C. attends the Army Gas School for a lecture.	WD

WAR DIARY
or
INTELLIGENCE SUMMARY

Army Form C. 2118

Page iv

B.E.F. July Antwerp. Month IV 1917

Place	Date	Hour	Summary of Events and Information	Remarks and references to Appendices
RENNINGHELST	25-4-17		Inspection of Gas Helmets, Iron Rations & Steel Helmets. One horse Ambulance left our N.C.O. i/c despatched with the 122nd Inf. Bde, in accordance with instructions contained in S.516.	WD
	26-4-17		Unsatisfactory Clinical notes, Veneral etc.	WD
	27-4-17		D.D.M.S. 10th Corps. visited A.D.M.S. inspected the Incinerator.	WD
	28-4-17		8 576 proceeds from A LINE.	
	30-4-17		A.482 recovered from A.D.M.S. with instructions to detail one man to report to X Corp. for a 2 weeks instruction in Signalling.	WD
			Pte EVANS E. proceeds to England on 6 Months in accordance with Instructions.	

Arthur Gartside RAMC
Lt Col O.C. 3rd Field Ambulance
D.C. 138

CONFIDENTIAL Vol 13

WAR DIARY

OF

138TH FIELD AMBULANCE

FROM MAY 1ST TO MAY 31ST, 1917.

(VOLUME V.)

COMMITTEE FOR THE
MEDICAL HISTORY OF THE WAR
Date 10 JUL 1917

WAR DIARY or INTELLIGENCE SUMMARY

Army Form C. 2118

138 Field Ambulance Vol. V Page 1. 1917

Place	Date	Hour	Summary of Events and Information	Remarks and references to Appendices
RENNINGHELST	1.5.17		63 O/Rs march to hospital. Inspected A&D DICKEBUSH and VOORMEZEELE R.A.P.	W28
	2.5.17		Pte Wilson F. Rane reports to 10 DMS XIX Corps for 14 days course of Instruction in Telephone Operator. (In accordance with A.D.M.S. instruction S. 482 d. 1/5/17). Ladret A.S.24 received from A.D.M.S	W28
	4.5.17		Short inspection of personnel – our factory – Ladret. Course of Instruction in Cookery.	W28
	5.5.17		Pte Powell H returns from Course of Instruction.	W28
	6.5.17		2 N.C.O's ordered to proceed to Second Army Rateside Coach for 14 days.	
	7.5.17		Whole Artillery active in neighbourhood. 7 A.W.S. – 23 wounded evacuated – Motor Ambulance car belonging to this unit damaged by shell fire. Two of the wounded cases in the car were killed in the Motor Ambulance. Two lying down cases slight wounds. The Motor Ambulance driver was also wounded, evacuated to C.C.S. The dismounted Ambulance was about wounded, evacuated to C.C.S. Brand in Winter clothing held. – President Capt T L E LAUDER R.AMC. Rane Members Capt CHESNEY and Capt WOODWARD R.A.M.C. Capt L.S ROCHE R.A.M.C. O/C working parties having been relieved by Capt CORK HILL R.A.M.C reported to H.Q for duty.	W29
	8.5.17		Gentle bombardment by the enemy of DICKEBUSH + Area East of OUDERDOM. – 25 wounded evacuated via C.C.S. through M.D.S	W28

WAR DIARY
or
INTELLIGENCE SUMMARY

Army Form C. 2118

Vol V
Page II
13th July Anhl 1917

Place	Date	Hour	Summary of Events and Information	Remarks and references to Appendices
RENNING HELST	11.5.17		Attended Conference at A.D.M.S.	WRS
	12.5.17		Capt. J. LONDON R.A.M.C. (T.C.) whilst temporarily with his unit prior to his departure for England, on expiration of contract.	WRS
			R.A.M.C. Opn. Order. 13. Copy No 7. received from the A.D.M.S.	WRS
	13.5.17		Capt J. LONDON R.A.M.C. (T.C.) proceeded. to England on expiration of contract. Relieves Underdown M.O.S. Westhoek A.D.S. WESTMEZEELE RD	WRS
	14.5.17		Capt A.C.T. WOODWARD R.A.M.C. relieves Lieut WALSH R.A.M.C. i/c. O/C. UNDERDOWN M.D.S. Lt WALSH R.A.M.C. reported to H.Q. for duty.	WRS
	15.5.17		R.A.M.C. D.O. No 14 Copy No 7. received from A.D.M.S. Party of 8 O.R details to proceed to A.D.S. for Ambulance work. Capt E. HUDSON R.A.M.C. (T.C.) and Lieut G. E. LLOYD R.A.M.C (T.C.) reported their arrival for temporary duty.	WRS
	16.5.17		A.D. Copy III received from 12th Bde. Secret d 5.24 Copy No 7. DO 110 Copy No 9 received from 12th Inf/Bde.	WRS

Army Form C. 2118

WAR DIARY
or
INTELLIGENCE SUMMARY
(Erase heading not required.)

138 Field Ambulance   Vol V 1917   Page 111

Place	Date	Hour	Summary of Events and Information	Remarks and references to Appendices
PENNINGHEUST	17.5.17		1 N.C.O, 5 O.R. A.S.C. (H.T.) with our G.S. wagon, one limber, no water cart and one horse ambulance, but 4 Bretonnias from 16 Tent Sub-Division left at 6.30 am to proceed with the transport of the 124th Inf Bdgs to the GANSPETTE area	WPG
"	18.5.17		Capt. W.F. WILSON. R.A.M.C. and 2 N.C.O.'s and remainder of "C" Section Tent Sub-division entrained at ABEELE station at 9.30 am with 16 124th Inf Bdgs for the GANSPETTE area (EPERLEQUES). 3 Motor Ambulance Cars (2 Sunbeams and 1 Ford) with Capt. L.S. ROCHE R.A.M.C left at 9.30 am for EPERLEQUES. Capt A.E.T. WOODWARD R.A.M.C. (T.e.) departed for duty with No. 13 C.C.S. Infectious OUDERDOM. M & S. A.S. DICKEBUSH. A.D.S. Allendes Infirmiere at N.U.M.I. Visited DICKEBUSH – no construction work.	WPG
"	21-5.17		2 N.C.O.'s returned from the Second Army seaside Camp and two N.C.O.'s proceeded to the Second Army Seaside Camp for 14 days.	WPG

WAR DIARY
or
INTELLIGENCE SUMMARY
(Erase heading not required.)

Army Form C. 2118

138th Field Ambulance Vol IV Part IV 1917

Place	Date	Hour	Summary of Events and Information	Remarks and references to Appendices
RENINGHELST	22.5.17		Units OUDERDOM & DICKEBUSH A.D.S. alterations to keeping the observation of the A.D.S. not regard to best cover almost complete. Northerlin receives from A.D.M.S. that Capt W.F. WILSON R.A.M.C. to take up the most has been posted as temporary M.O. i/c 26th Royal Fusiliers.	WDS
	23-5-17		OO 110 Copy 18 received from 122nd Inf. Bde. Do 87 " 19 " " 123rd " Capt R.T. HERDMAN R.A.M.C. reports his annual leave from No 5 O.C. C.S. finally. Allotted conference at A.D.M.S. S 53.9 and 53.5 (2) received from A.D.M.S.	WDS
	25-5-17		Allotted sheet maps(?) sheet 28 Poperinghe	WDS
	26-5-17		Capt A.E. KNIGHT R.A.M.C. posted to 39th Div. and struck off strength. Although accompanying Capt. W. CHESNEY R.A.M.C.(S.R.) reports his arrival for duty on relinquishing charge of that Div. Batts. all the R.A.M.C. personnel reported from the Batts. formerly with the exception of this O.R's.	WDS
	27-5-17		Capt R.T. HERDMAN R.A.M.C. proceeds to RUDERDOM wood for duty. Enemy shelled tent area as one 60 wounder Fournier Miny.	
	28-5-17		Amongst two dug outs for loafers at the A.D.S. letterences struck hit — one was damaged — but the other undamaged, although the envelope thrown clear of the ground the aeroplane the refreshen	WDS

WAR DIARY
or
INTELLIGENCE SUMMARY

Army Form C. 2118

138th Field Ambulance Vol V Page 5 1917

Place	Date	Hour	Summary of Events and Information	Remarks and references to Appendices
RENNINGHELST	28-5-17		Heavy hostile shelling of back area with gas shells & lim shells. 7 R.A.M.C. personnel belonging to this unit wounded — 5 at VIERSTRAETEELB R.A.P. W. 2 at M.A.D.S. Over 70 wounded evacuated during through. C.O. 88 C/Spy. 17 from 123 Bde. received.	WRG
	29-5-17		Casualties heavy through day through night — 90 wounded — C.O. 55 Capt. 10 received from 122 wBdyr. Capt. W. CHESNEY R.A.M.C. & Capt. LUMLEY R.A.M.C. relieved Cpt. LLOYD R.A.M.C. & Lt. WALSH R.A.M.C. at A.D.S.	WRG
	30-5-17		Hand notice — On whole de wounded. S. 545 received for A.D.M.S. D.O. 113 C/Spy 18 received from 122 Inf Bdyr. C.O. 90 C/Spy 20 received from 123 Inf Bdyr. Jnr. 12 midnight. W.D 12 midnight 30/5/17. 41 wounded through the A.D.S.	WRG
	31-5-17		During the week 5 men were evacuated as casualties. A's & acid. L. 547 & 57.9 received from A.D.M.S. Shelled with shrapnel during through week. very good.	WRG

W.R. Grayson
Lt Col R.A.M.C.
O.C. 138" Field Ambulance

CONFIDENTIAL

WAR DIARY OF

138TH FIELD AMBULANCE. R.A.M.C.

FROM :- JUNE 1st 1917.   TO :- JUNE 30TH 1917.

VOLUME VI

APPENDIX "C" (Continued).

LIMBER No. 2.

SHELL DRESSINGS.	12 Haversacks.
STRETCHERS.	12.
BLANKETS.	30.
GROUND SHEETS.	30.
SOYERS STOVE.	1.
OXO BOXES.	1.
TEA BOXES.	1.
SUGAR BOXES.	1.

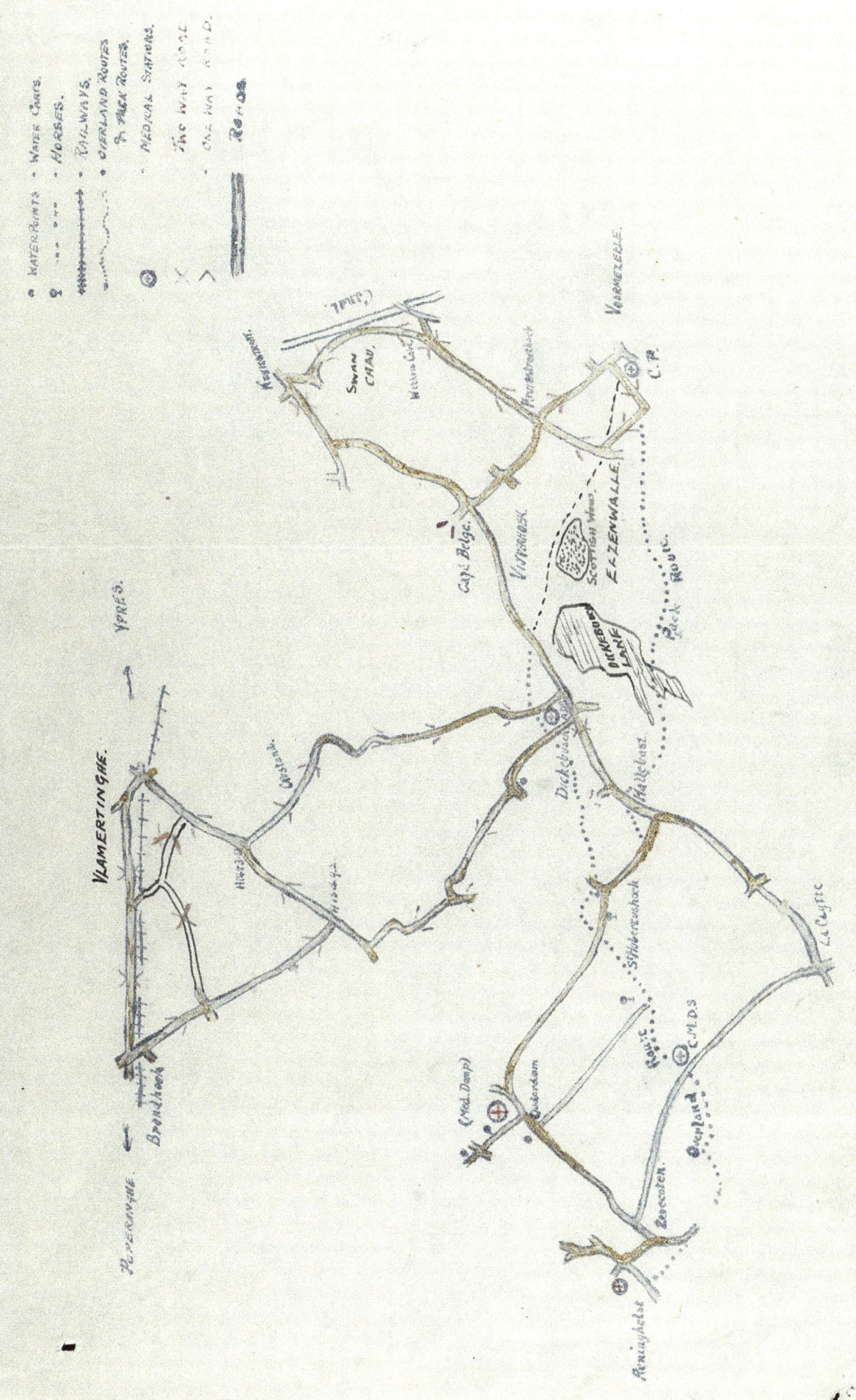

Army Form C. 2118

WAR DIARY
or
INTELLIGENCE SUMMARY
(Erase heading not required.)

Vol VI PAGE 1 1917

Place	Date	Hour	Summary of Events and Information	Remarks and references to Appendices
Pennyfelt	1/6/17		In Hospital 1 Officer 52 O.R. Attended conference at A.D.M.S. at 10 a.m. Hunt Monthly Inspection of Personnel 1760. Proceeded on leave to England from 2/5 - 12/5 Conference held re Officers Mess for all M.O.'s of Div. Sgt a.D.M.S at 5.30 p.m. Received 55 & 9 & 530 from a D.M.S. Wounded admitted from midnight 3/5 to midnight 1/5 Off 2 O.R. 68.	M&S
	2/6/17		In Hospital 1 Off 64 O.R. Appendices 1a. No.7 No.11 & 75 11 a & 0.0.88 from 123 Bdl received also continuation of appendix 11. Rec'd 3552 from A.D.M.S. Casualties admitted from midnight 1/6/17 to midnight 2/5 Off. nil O.R.'s 26.	M&S
	3/6/17		75 O.R. in Hospital 5 5148 received from A.D.M.S. Casualties admitted from midnight 2/5 to midnight 3/5 Off 3 O.R 42	M&S
	4/6/17		3 Off 74 O.R. in Hospital Received 3555 & 5457 from A.D.M.S re revised French Codes O.O. No.16 Copy No.1 Received from ADMS re evacuation of Hospital. O.O. No.17 " " " O.O. No.118 received from 122nd Inf. Bde. Casualties admitted from midnight 3/5 to mid 4/5 Off 3 O.R. 46. Issued Operation order 1 – 10 op to 7.30 p.m.	M&S

Army Form C. 2118

WAR DIARY
or
INTELLIGENCE SUMMARY
(Erase heading not required.)

VOLUME VI PAGE 7

Instructions regarding War Diaries and Intelligence Summaries are contained in F.S. Regs., Part II. and the Staff Manual respectively. Title Pages will be prepared in manuscript.

Place	Date	Hour	Summary of Events and Information	Remarks and references to Appendices
Reninghelst	5/6/17	10.0 a.m.	Attended conference at A.D.M.S. Transport Coln in Hofstät to D.R.S. o.666 & handed over H.P. Building to 73rd F.A. (on acceptance with A.D.M.S. Hut Box. B.O. No.16. of 4/5) Relief completed by 6.0 p.m. All personnel of this Unit proceeded to Ouderdom (Sheet 28 NW 9.30 c.4.8.) Wounded admitted to said for forwarding after off 2 O.R.H.	W.O.S. /
Ouderdom 9.30 C.4.8.	6/6/17	6.9 p.m.	Received O.C. No 1. Bear F.A. from Freres sub divisions Lieut B. & Seagal R.A.M.C. proceeded on temporary M.O. 76 23rd Middx Regt. 2 Bearer Sub divs of this Unit departed at noon to forward to Collecting Post Voormezeele also 1 Tent sub divisions Capt. R J Hudson R.A.M.C. proceeded to 5 Corps Prisoner of War Camp for duty. O.O's from 139th & 110th F.A.'s received Remainder of unit with exception of 1 Tent sub div & Re O.M. proceeded to A.D.S. Dickebusch (H.27. d.4.8) where Hughes were established Reported to A.D.M.S. that Field Ambulance were in position allotted as under H.Qs. A.D.S. {A" Bearer & "A" Section Tent Sub division Collecting Post Voormezeele {B" & "C" Section Bearer Sub divisions Full detail in O.O./No. 4 Copy No.2. attached Medical Group Ouderdom 13" Section	See APPENDIX "A"
"	7/6/17		See appendix "B" Report of operations. CAPT. E HUDSON, R.A.M.C. forwarded as temp. M.O. % 15th Hants Regt. O.O. No 18 received from A.D.M.S.	See APPENDIX "B"

Army Form C. 2118

WAR DIARY
or
INTELLIGENCE SUMMARY
(Erase heading not required.)

VOLUME VI PAGE 111

Place	Date	Hour	Summary of Events and Information	Remarks and references to Appendices
Ouderdom	8th		Field Ambulance returned to Ouderdom (Medical Dump). Lieut V.M. Walsh, RAMC. Proceeded to WATOU in relief of Capt. Browne RAMC as M.O.i/c Corps Dist. Supply Column. (In accordance with ADMS S570). Capt Molyneux RAMC & 5.O.R proceeded to WELLINGTON JUNCTION in relief of Capt Browne RAMC & 5.O.R. received staff from ADMS 2nd Div.	MG
"	9th		Capt Roberts RAMC & 25.O.R. proceeded to C.P. Voormezeele (2nd Div). Medical & Sanitary arrangements made for 187 Bde RFA, 9/90 Bde RFA (& D/190 Bde RFA) Wagon lines, also H.Q. Wagon lines of 190 Bde RFA. (ADMS S476 & 577)	MG
"	10th		Received instructions from ADMS that 2 M.O.s & 25 O.R. of 1st Corps would be relieved. Capt. E.A. Lumby 137th F.A. & 25.O.R. proceeded to C.P. Voormezeele in relief of Capt Roberts RAMC & 25.O.R. who returned to this H.Q. 1 M.O. & 8 men proceeded to Wellington Junction in relief of Capt Molyneux RAMC & 5 O.R. who returned to this H.Q. Received Medical arrangements from ADMS 2nd Div stating revert to normal from 3.0 am 11/9/17. 2 Bearer sub divisions of 139th Field Ambulance returned to their Unit in accordance with ADMS S571. S572 received from ADMS.	MG

WAR DIARY
or
INTELLIGENCE SUMMARY
(Erase heading not required.)

Army Form C. 2118

VOLUME VI PAGE IV.

Place	Date	Hour	Summary of Events and Information	Remarks and references to Appendices
Onderdom	11th.	9.00 a.m	2 Officers & 25 O.R. of T. Corps departed to report to their Unit.	
		2.9 p.m	Transport of 140th Field Ambulance returned to Unit.	
			O.O. No 9 Copy No 1 received from a.D.M.S. 41st Div. (Relief of 24th by 47th Div.) (See appendix "C" attached).	See Appendix "C"
		7.39 p.m	O.O No 5 Copies 1-10 issued.	
			O.O No 23 received from 140th Field Ambulance	
			Capt L.S.G. Roots R.A.M.C, 2 Bearer Sub-divisions "A" & "B" Sec. & "A" Section Tent Sub-division proceeded to a.D.S.	
			In accordance with Medical arrangements 41st Div detachments of this Unit as in O.O. No 4 returned to this Unit: also 1 N.C.O. & T.O.R from WELLINGTON JUNCTION.	W.R.S.
	12th		"C" Section Bearer Sub-division proceeded to A.D.S. Voormezeele.	
			Visited Aid Posts & A.D.S. with Capt J.L.J. Lander and arranged the evacuation of cases of 122nd Bde. in accordance with O.O No 5. (Appendix "C" attached).	
			Received Medical Arrangements in accordance with I Corps from a.D.M.S. Warning order received from A.D.M.S. of evacuation of Camp at Onderdom. To be completed by 6 o/p.m. 13th June.	W.R.S.

Army Form C. 2118

WAR DIARY
or
INTELLIGENCE SUMMARY

VOLUME VI   PAGE V

(Erase heading not required.)

Place	Date	Hour	Summary of Events and Information	Remarks and references to Appendices
Ouderdom	13th		Visited Advd Posts & A.D.S. Vacated Camp at Ouderdom & proceeded to Sheet 28 S.W. N.3 d.3.8 HALLEBAST CORNER, & reported position to A.D.M.S. at 6 p.m.	
HALLEBAST CORNER (28 S.W. N3 d.3.8)	"		Received S.596 (4th Div. O.O No.133) from A.D.M.S. Received S.584 (Secret Codes instruction) also S.582 (Movee Hut Div) from A.D.M.S. 1 O.R. of this Unit evacuated wounded. Issued O.O. No. 6. Copies 1-10. (all Appendix "D" attached)	WDS
-"-	14th		Received O.O. No 120 Copy 15 from 122nd Inf. Bde. H.Q. moved to A.D.S. Voormezeele for above operations. Casualties admitted from 9 p.m. 14th — 8.30 a.m. 15/6/17 – Officers 4. O.R. 152 Prisoners of War 8. Report on operations as attached Appendix E. 1 R.A.M.C. personal wounded (not evacuated)	WDS
-"-	15th		Attended conference at A.D.M.S. at 11 a.m. H.Q. retd to N3 d.3.8. O.O. No 122 Copy No 13 received from 122nd Bde. Lt. Walsh R.A.M.C. reported his arrival back for duty Enemy counter-attack during night. 2 Horse Ambulance & H.G.S. Wagons (commuted) sent to A.D.S. for duty if required. 2 Horse Amb. & 1 G.S. Wagon returned at 4.30 a.m. 16th not further required. Total casualties passing through A.D.S. from 7 p.m. – 7 p.m. Off. 6 O.R. 79 P.of.W. nil. 16/17	WRG

Army Form C. 2118

WAR DIARY
or
INTELLIGENCE SUMMARY
(Erase heading not required.)

VOLUME VI   PAGE VI

Place	Date	Hour	Summary of Events and Information	Remarks and references to Appendices
HALLEBAST CORNER	16th		LIEUT. V.M WALSH R.A.M.C. proceeded to 72nd A.F.A. as temporary M.O.H. vice LT. JUDSON, R.A.M.C. (Authority A.D.M.S 161st d 15th) Received S.590 from A.D.M.S. (Correction to Code) Casualties admitted from 7.0 p.m - 7.0 a.m. 17/6/17 Off H. O.R. 60.	W.O.9.
"	17th		78362 Pte McLEAN. J & 74046 Pte HURST, H.T. of this unit killed in action at 26th Royal Irishers Aid Post in Dametrosse 0.9 c.6.5. and 76500 Pte Mills. J wounded evacuated to C.C.S during the early morning. 1 O.R wounded during afternoon. Received S.593 from A.D.M.S stating that 1 Barber Sub-division from 140th F.A. had been instructed to report for duty. On arrival this bearer division proceeded to A.D.S Voormezele.	W.O.
"	18th		Capt. Jno F. LAUDER D.S.O.M.C. R.A.M.C. proceeded on leave to England from 18/6/17 – 28/6/17 O.O No.123 received from 122nd Infantry Bde.	W.O.
"	19th		Hostile shelling in vicinity of camp between 6.7 a.m. 1 wounded from adjoining camp admitted, evacuated to Main Dressing Station. No casualties to R.A.M.C personnel. Capt. R.T Herdman R.A.M.C. proceeded as M.O.H. (temporary) 72nd Bde A.F.A vice LIEUT. V.M WALSH R.A.M.C. evacuated sick (A.D.M.S letter M.1 d 18th) Medical & Sanitary arrangements of 193rd Lab. Coy at N5 c Central arranged in accordance with A.D.M.S S.595 d 18th.	W.O.

WAR DIARY
or
INTELLIGENCE SUMMARY
(Erase heading not required.)

Army Form C. 2118

VOLUME VI PAGE VII.

Place	Date	Hour	Summary of Events and Information	Remarks and references to Appendices
HALLEBAST CORNER.	20th		Hostile Shelling in vicinity of Camp. (No R.A.M.C. Casualties) Proceeded to A.D.S. and stayed during night.	W.R.
"	21st	12-1-0am 9.40am	Hostile Shelling of Camp. 1 O.R. Killed & 1 O.R. slightly wounded of this Unit. D.A.D.M.S. visited A.D.S. Vormezeele re vacation of White Chateau. D.A.A. & Q.M.G. 41st Div visited H.Q. to investigate a new site for H.Q. of this Unit. Received S.599 from a D.M.S. stating that H.Q. were to be situated at Sheet 28 S.W. N.1.d.2.2.	W.R.
" Nr LA CLYTTE N1.d.2.2.	22nd		Vacated Camp at N3.d.3.8 & proceeded to N.1.d.2.2. Reported situation & completion of move at 10pm to A.D.M.S. Capt. L.W. BAIN, R.A.M.C. reported for duty & proceeded to A.D.S. Vormezeele.	W.R.
"	23rd		Received Warning Order No 5. Copy No 15 from 122nd Bde re relief of Div. Received Warning Order S603 from A.D.M.S. 41st Div.	W.R.

WAR DIARY
or
INTELLIGENCE SUMMARY

Army Form C. 2118

VOLUME VI   PAGE VIII

(Erase heading not required.)

Place	Date	Hour	Summary of Events and Information	Remarks and references to Appendices
NR LA CLYTTE N.1.d.2.2	24th		Received S.607 from A.D.M.S. (Billeting). CAPT. L.W. BAIN proceeded as temporary M.O. to "Queen's" R.W. Surrey Regt. in accordance with A.D.M.S. instructions. 1 N.C.O. & 1 O.R. proceeded to report to 122nd Bde. Billeting Officer.	W.B.
"	25th		Received S.610 from A.D.M.S. (This Brigade.) (Billeting scheme & map of area to be occupied by this Bde.) Received O.O. No 20 from A.D.M.S. (Relief. also Medical arrangements) Issued O.O. No. (Copies 1–12. (See appendix "F" attached (Copy No 2).	W.B.
"	26th		Received Map of new area, in accordance with O.O. No 20 received from A.D.M.S. Received S.602 from A.D.M.S. and arranged Medical Care of 9th Canadian Cty. Insp. Bde. in accordance with instructions. O.C. 4th London Field Ambulance visited H.Q. & proceeded with O.C. of this Unit to A.D.S. Vormezeele. Scheme of evacuation of casualties from line to A.D.S. fully explained. Wounded men in working.	W.B.

1875 Wt. W 593/826 1,000,000 4/15 J.B.C. & A. A.D.S.S./Forms/C. 2118.

WAR DIARY or INTELLIGENCE SUMMARY

Army Form C. 2118

VOLUME VI   PAGE IX

Place	Date	Hour	Summary of Events and Information	Remarks and references to Appendices
Nr LA CLYTTE N.1.d.2.2	27th	9.0am	1 Officer & 1 Bearer Sub division of 16th London Field Ambulance arrived at H.Q. & proceeded to A.D.S. for distribution to various Aid-posts. Further relief parties arrived during the day & proceeded to A.D.S. Received amendments & additions to A.D.M.S. O.O No 20. (This F.A. on relief to proceed to W.S.C. & take over from 41st Field Ambulance). O.O.No.124 Copy No.15 received from 122nd Inf Bde. (Relief of Brigade)	WD
-"-	28th	9.0am	Relief of this Field Ambulance completed. Field Ambulance & transport proceeded at 10.30 a.m. by march table, & arrived at W.S.C. 3.9 at 3.30p.m. Reported position & arrival at 4.0pm to A.D.M.S. 41st Division. Personnel accommodated in huts for night, as 41st F.A. did not move until morning of 29th.	WD
-"-	29th		A.D.M.S & D.A.D.M.S. 41st Div. visited camp.	WD
-"-	30th		Strength of Unit R.A.M.C. A.S.C.-M.T A.S.C-M.T Officers 9. OR 178. OR 32 OR 12	

W Ross Garrett
Lieut Cy RAMC
Commanding 138th Field Ambulance

APPENDIX "C"

MINIMUM EQUIPMENT FOR AN ADVANCED DRESSING STATION.

LIMBER No. 1.

PANNIER "F"	Complete, ONE.
PANNIER "T"	" ONE.
FIELD MEDICAL PANNIER.	No. 1.
FIELD SURGICAL PANNIER.	No. 1.
MEDICAL COMFORT PANNIER.	1.
SURGICAL HAVERSACKS.	3
MEDICAL COMPANION.	1.
BUTCHERS SET.	1.
ENTRENCHING TOOL BAG. (COMPLETE)	1.
POLES FOR PENDANT FLAG.	4.
TOW SURGEONS.	10 lbs.
LAMPS HURRICANE. (In addition to 2 in "F" Pannier)	2.
STOVE, OIL, PRIMUS.	1.
RED FAN.	1.
PARAFFIN.	5 Gallons.
CRESOL.	1 Gallon.
RESERVE DRESSING BOX.	1 "
BUCKETS, CANVAS.	2.
OPERATING TABLE.	1.
" " (CUSHION FOR).	1.
BOTTLES, WATER.	3.
BOX CONTAINING STATIONERY.	1.
OFFICE TABLE.	1.
OXYGEN CYLINDER.	1.
FEEDER. (IN "F" PANNIER).	2.
FUNNEL TIN.(" "). ½ pint.	1.
KETTLE, ENAMELLED (In "F" Pannier).	1.
BASINS, 11" ("F" Pannier).	2.
" 14" ("H" Pannier).	2.
BRUSHES, SCRUBBING. ("F" Pannier).	3.
PANNIKINS PINT ("H" Pannier).	12.
METHYLATED SPIRIT. ("F" Pannier)	1 tin.
LAMPS, OPERATING.	1.
TOWELS " ("H" Pannier)	3.
ANTI-TETANIC SERUM. ("F" Pannier)	1 box.
" " SYRINGE.	1.
TRESSLES.	2.

/ No. 2 Limber.

Appendix "A". 138 F.A.
June 1917.
2

138th. FIELD AMBULANCE. R.A.M.C. OPERATION ORDER NO--

1. NARRATIVE: The 41st. Division occupying the ST. ELOI sector
have the 47TH. Division and 1 th. Division on their right and left
respectively, and will be disposed as follows:-
    Two Infantry Brigades will be in the front line, the ....
one left and 1 other on the right. The 3 Bde. Inf. Bde. will be in
reserve.

2. BOUNDARIES OF THE 41st. DIVISION.
Right: OOSTHOVE ALM from .... including DEAD
DOG Farm but excluding .... edge on ....
Road dividing Southern extremity of DICKEBUSCH LAKE.
Left: JUNCTION TRENCHES .... SPOIL BANK Road -
OOSTHOVE FM - REGENT ST. ....
....
to Cafe Belge.

3. BATTLE HEADQUARTERS this Unit will be at A.D.S. DICKEBUSCH at and
after Zero - 4. Before this hour at OUDERDOM.

4. DISTRIBUTION OF R.A.M.C. OFFICERS & PERSONNEL in th. Field AMBCE.
(a) Capt. J. Litt, Bearer Officer i/c Stretcher bearers. ....
Dump, and bearer sub-divisions of "B" "C" "D" sections will proceed
.... VOORMEZEELE and take over the line of evacuation between
R.A.P. and C.P.
(b) Capt. W.M. Chesney .... i/c Capt .... and rest sub-
divisions of "C" Section will take over and establish a COLLECTING
POST at VOORMEZEELE.
(c) Capt. .... i/c and Lieut. .... and "D" Section rest sub-
division will take over A.D.S. DICKEBUSCH and all stores and
equipment.
(d) All Mob. stores and equipment at OUDERDOM i.e. Medical Dump
will be packed and stored without delay and compliance reported
to Officer Commanding this Unit.
(e) Men Sub-division "B" Section will proceed under Lt. ....
to MOB. DUMP OUDERDOM (formerly M.D.S.) All Officers of this
Unit not already detailed, will proceed on evacuation of the
Hospital, REMINGHELST, to this station and await instructions there.
(f) On handing over at A.D.S. & M.D.S. OUDERDOM, relieved parties
will stand fast, pending receipt of orders as to their further
movements and precise instructions regarding the disposition of
their personnel.
(g) HOSPITAL BUILDING, REMINGHELST - will be completely evacuated
of sick, before handing over.
(h) BEARER SUB-DIVISION "A" Section will supply all personnel to
fill vacancies in the other sub-divisions caused by requirements
of Medical N.C.O's and men from bearers .... Bearers at A.D.S.
(i) 139th. & 140th. FIELD AMBULANCES. Officers accompanying and
the Bearer sub-divisions of these two Field Ambulances will
rendezvous at MEDICAL DUMP, OUDERDOM. The Senior Officer 138th.
present will report immediately to Officer Commanding this Unit on
Arrival. Strength of these sub-divisions and Officers as follows.

AMB.	Med. Dump		O.P.		C.P.		A.D.S.	
	Officers	sub-div	Off.	sub-div	Off.	sub-div	Off.	sub-div
138.								
	2		K+M		4		1	2
		2						1
140th		2		2				

6. TRANSPORT. The allocation of wheeled stretchers, motor cyclists and evacuating transport, constituted as under, will be as follows:-

	UNIT				DISPOSITION	
	138th.	139th.	140th.	Total.	"Y" day in position.	"Z" day (& from).
1. Motor Amb'cs.	4.	6.	7.	17.	3 in line 10 nr Cabstand) H.7.c.2.8.)	5 from C.P.
2. Horse Amb'cs.	3.	3.	3.	9.	9 Med. Dump.	9 from A.D.S.
3. G.S. Wagons. (converted)	4.	6.	5.	15.	15 Med. Dump	8 from C.P. 7 " A.D.S.
4. Wheeled Stretchers.	7.	4.	4.	15.	7 C.P. 8 A.D.S. (reserve)	2 from A.D.S. 13 " C.P.
5. Motor Cyclists.	2.			2.	1 A.D.S. 1 Ouderdom.	1 A.D.S. 1 Ouderdom.

All other transport of this Unit (& "B" Section "A.D.S. Limber") will rendezvous and continue to be parked at Medical Dump, Ouderdom.

A reliable man will be attached to the 10 Motor Ambulances stationed at the CABSTAND, whose duty will be to receive and transmit to the N.C.O. of this Units Motor Ambulances, all telephone messages received from A.D.S.

7. EVACUATION.

(1) From VOORMEZEELE C.P. to DICKEBUSCH A.D.S. by a continuation of the following means of transport :- Div. Motor Ambulances, Horse Ambulances, G.S. Wagons (converted), wheeled stretchers or trolley, as occasion may require or necessity dictate.
WALKING WOUNDED will proceed by overland track or by the VOORMEZEELE - KRUISSTRAATHOEK - CAFE BELGE ROAD back to A.D.S. DICKEBUSCH, direct without touching at C.P. A control post will be established at junction of overland routes to direct such cases to A.D.S.
H.Q. Dickebusch will be informed from time to time by this the Officer i/c C.P. of the number of cases, approximately, and whether sitting or lying, requiring evacuation. This information will be in writing and be conveyed as far as possible by down going ambulances; otherwise and when deemed necessary by telephone or runner.
(2) FROM A.D.S.
SERIOUSLY WOUNDED FROM A.D.S. DICKEBUSCH To C.M.D.S. for Seriously Wounded at BRANDHOEK by Divisional Cars.
(3) LIGHTLY WOUNDED cases to C.M.D.S. for "Lightly Wounded" at Prisoner of War Camp LA CLYTTE Road, by Divisional Cars.

8. CLASSIFICATION & DISTRIBUTION OF WOUNDED.

(a) All cases will be divided at C.P. & A.D.S. into SERIOUSLY WOUNDED (Lying down) or SLIGHTLY WOUNDED (sitting & walking). Lightly wounded will, however, be subdivided at C.P. into "Sitting" & "Walking". Sitting cases will be conveyed from C.P. to A.D.S. by G.S. Wagons or Horse Ambulances. Walking cases will, however, make their way by road or overland tracks to the latter station. Southward bound empty lorries on CAFE BELGE - DICKEBUSCH Road will be stopped in Dickebusch village by means of Red Flags by day and lamps at night and used to convey walking wounded to C.M.D.S. for Lightly Wounded at La Clytte. These parties should be accompanied by a R.A.M.C. Orderly who will be in possession of a nominal roll of cases, shewing destination. This roll will be handed over at C.M.D.S. and the orderly return as quickly as possible to A.D.S. On no account will lorries be unnecessarily delayed in carrying out this method of evacuation. Motor Ambulances will as far as possible be employed in evacuating lying cases fro

A.D.S. and from the latter station to C.M.D.S. for Seriously Wounded at BRANDHOEK.

    (b) MORIBUND CASES will not be evacuated.

    (c) ABDOMINAL, HEAD or CHEST, to BRANDHOEK.

    (d) WOUNDED PRISONERS OF WAR, also SELF-INFLICTED wounded (whether intentional or accidental) accompanied by details and F.M. Card clearly marked "S.I.", to La Clytte or Brandhoek. "Sitting Lightly Wounded", when necessary and when it is possible can be evacuated in converted G.S. wagons from C.P.

    (e) SICK OF FIELD AMBULANCE PERSONNEL to D.R.S.

    (f) GASSED CASES to F.A. WARATAH CAMP (on main RENINGHELST-POP; Rd)

    (g) SHELL SHOCK cases to C.M.D.S. for Seriously Wounded

9. In all cases in which MORPHIA is given, "M" will be clearly marked on the forehead of the recipient with an indelible ink pencil, and the usual entries made on the F.M. Card. i.e. dose given and time of administration. The F.M. Card will be attached to the patients in all cases, where Morphia is given at the C.P.

10. RECORDS. Nominal Rolls will be kept only at A.D.S. and 41st Div. Casualties recorded separately from other divisions, and Officers from Other Ranks. Disposal and usual details only will be required.

11. SITUATION REPORTS. will be rendered as often as possible by O.C's. i/c C.P. A.D.S. and Forward Bearers.

12. TELEPHONES.
From Signal Exchange, C.P. VOORMEZEELE to :-
    (a) R.A.P's directly.
    (b) Brigade H.Q.
    (c) A.D.S.
    (d) Through A.D.S. to Medical Dump Ouderdom.
the special details (re Appendix "A") details detached from their sections for duty as Telephonists at C.P. A.D.N. & Ouderdom, will be responsible for the transmission of all messages, and that these, whether received or emitted are immediately taken in writing on the proper forms and transmitted to those concerned without delay.

13. FIELD MEDICAL CARDS. (A.F.W. 3118). All cases evacuated from A.D.S. will have this A.F. attached, and all entries revelant and referrable to a Field Ambulance in it, will duly filled in.

14. BATTLE CASUALTY WIRES from H.Q. Dickebusch, will be despatched to reach A.D.M.S. Office by 3-0 a.m. 12 noon & 9-0 p.m. for their respective periods.
USUAL CASUALTY WIRE affecting R.A.M.C. personnel (& A.S.C. attached made up from noon to noon will be sent to 41st Div. "A" and repeated to A.D.M.S. Office. Officer i/c C.P. & Worward Bearers will inform H.Q. Dickebusch immediately, of any casualties occurring in their commands, stating Units, e.g. 139th. F.A. together with usual other details. O.C. 139th. & 140th. F.A.'s will be informed of all such casualties occurring in the personnel of their Units. Casualties occurring in other Units will not be included in this Units Casualty wire.

15. ANTI-TETANIC SERUM will not be given.

16. WATER.
    (a) Water Carts will be attached as follows :-
        "A" Section water cart   A.D.S. DICKEBUSCH.
        "B"   "   "   "   MEDICAL DUMP. OUDERDOM.
        "C"   "   "   "   at DICKEBUSCH in reserve for C.P.
                                                if necessary

16. PETROL TINS. 150 - 2 Gallon Tins will be distributed from the Medical Dump as under :-
   (1) 80 to Officer i/c Forward Bearers - 40 to R.A.P's (10 each) and the same number of refills (for exchange) at VOORMEZEELE
   (2) 70 held in reserve at C.P. at disposal of Officer i/c forward bearers.
   (c) SOURCES OF WATER SUPPLY IN VOORMEZEELE OR ITS VICINITY.
       (1) Water Point at I.31.d.5.9. where petrol tins can be filled from stand pipes. Other means are available at this point for filling of water carts etc.,
       (2) TWO WELLS IN VOORMEZEELE itself -
           (a) Brewery Well at I.31.c.3.5.
           (b) Well in Village square. I.31.a.3.4.
       2 scoops of Chlorinated Lime meets amount of chlorination required
       (3) Subsequently it is probable the following points as sources of water supply will be available :-
           (a) Moated Grange.
           (b) Dome House.
       (4) Water points for water carts.
                                                   G.29.a.7.5.
       (5)   "   "   " horses.   H.31.b.54.3.
                                                   G.33.b.4.2.

17. ARMS, Public Equipment, ammunition etc., will be handed over if required to the nearest Stragglers' Post to re-equip stragglers, otherwise they will be accumulated and handed over to the representative of D.A.D.O.S.

18. REVOLVERS, FIELD GLASSES, WIRECUTTERS, COMPASSES, WATCHES etc., will be taken from wounded admitted at A.D.S. (D.A.D.O.S. will arrange to collect them periodically.)

19. BATTLE STRAGGLERS' POSTS.
    KRUISSTRAATHOEK.   H.30.d.3.1.
    HALLEBAST CORNER.   H.32.d.7½.0.
    DICKEBUSCH.   H.35.b.6.9.
       All N.C.O's and men reporting sick or wounded unnecessarily at A.D.S. or C.P. will be handed over to the nearest Battle Straggler Post, and nominal rolls of all such cases should be kept. A Police N.C.O. stationed at C.P. will be responsible that particulars of N.C.O's and men arriving at this post without arms and equipment, whose wound is so slight as not to justify loss or abandonment of such, is taken and reported.

20. EQUIPMENT SLINGS, BEARERS. All bearers with the exception of the 2 sub-divisions of the 135th. F.A. mentioned in para 4 (a), will proceed up the line less valise (and greatcoat i.e. skeleton equipment, ground sheet may, however be retained, if required. Slings will be issued at Ouderdom, and these will be retained by him during the whole of the subsequent operations and be regarded as part and parcel of his equipment, and will be carried looped through the shoulder strap.

21. WHEELED STRETCHERS. 6 wheeled stretchers will be stationed at the C.P. All others available will be stationed at DICKEBUSCH (in reserve).

22. MAP REFERENCES.
    M.D.S. RENINGHELST.
    MEDICAL DUMP. OUDERDOM.
    A.D.S. DICKEBUSCH.
    Collecting Post. VOORMEZEELE.
    C.C.S. for Lightly Wounded at P. of W. Camp.
    C.C.S. for Seriously Wounded at BRANDHOEK.
    ADVANCED MOTOR AMBULANCE WORKSHOPS. LINDE HOEK Fm.
    CARSTAND.

ROAD CIRCUITS.

(1) EASTERN (Circuit between A.D.S. & C.P. VOORMEZEELE).

DICKEBUSCH – CAFE BELGE – KRUISSTRAATHOEK – ELZENWALLE – KRUISSTRAATHOEK thence N.E. to WITHUIS CABARET and then by new switch road running N.E. round van Chateau leaving Chateau on left and canal on right hand, to main Dickebusch – Cafe Belge – Ypres Road – to A.D.S.

Tracks & Overland Routes.

(a) A pack track extends from VOORMEZEELE, westwards to DICKEBUSCH – LA CLYTTE Road which it meets in neighbourhood of HALLEBAST.
(b) An overland track extends from A.D.S. to a point just N. of DICKEBUSCH VILLAGE, on DICKEBUSCH – CAFE BELGE main road.
This track continues overland N. of Dickebusch Lake and Scottish Wood to Elzenwalle, thence by Elzenwalle – Voormezeele Road to C.P. or by Middlesex Lane & Voormezeele Road to C.P. or for up traffic by Victoria Street. Victoria Street is an "up" trench and must on no account be used for wounded.

(2) S.W. CIRCUIT (between A.D.S. & C.M.D.S. for L.W. LA CLYTTE).

DICKEBUSCH via HALLEBAST CORNER by LA CLYTTE – DICKEBUSCH – CAFE BELGE Road to LA CLYTTE and along LA CLYTTE – ZEVECOTEN – RENINGHELST Road to C.M.D.S. for L.W. Return via ZEVECOTEN to OUDERDOM by OUDERDOM – HALLEBAST to DICKEBUSCH by LA CLYTTE – DICKEBUSCH Road to A.D.S.

An overland route extends from A.D.S. to LA CLYTTE C.M.D.S., HALLEBAST CORNER can be avoided by western termination of VOORMEZEELE – HALLEBAST pack route.

(3) N.W. CIRCUIT (Between A.D.S. & C.M.D.S. for S.W. BRANDHOEK).

From A.D.S. past R.E. Dump and MILLE-KAPELLE Fm. to OUDERDOM – VLAMERTINGHE Road. By this latter to VLAMERTINGHE, along main VLAMERTINGHE – POPERINGHE road to BRANDHOEK C.M.D.S.
Return by road extending from BRANDHOEK to H.13.d.9.2. thence N.E. by OUDERDOM – VLAMERTINGHE ROAD to H.14.b.3.8. southwards to DICKEBUSCH.
Track (a) para (1) will be used if necessary by all wheeled traffic other than Motor Ambulances, returning from VOORMEZEELE.
Track (b) para (1) will be used for walking wounded.

24. ACKNOWLEDGE.

Issued at 8-30 p.m.
June 4th., 1917.

W Ross Gardner
Lt. Col. R.A.M.C.
Commanding 138th. Field Ambulance.

Copy No. 1. File.
2. War Diary.
3. A.D.M.S. 41st Div.
4. O.C. 138th. F.A.
5. O.C. 140th. F.A.
6. O.C. 73rd. F.A.
7. Spare.
8. Spare
9. Spare
10. Spare.

APPENDICES.

"A" Special duties N.C.O's and men.
"B" Medical Comforts and Stores.
"C" Equipment and stores of sectional "A.D.S. LIMBER"
"D" Map – Traffic Routes.

APPENDIX "A"

SPECIAL DUTIES N.C.O's and men.

1. Telephonists.

2. Clerks.

3. R.E. Clerks.

4. Cooks.

5. Water.

6. N.C.O. i/c evacuation A.D.S.

7. N.C.O. i/c A.S.C. evacuation horse transport.

8. Wagon & Amb'c's Orderlies (Converted G.S. evacuating)

9. Q.M. Stores.

138 F.A. June 1917.

APPENDIX "B"

	MED. DUMP. (Res.)	A.D.S.	C.P.	4 R.A.P's. (Each)	Total R.A.P's.	GRAND TOTAL.	
(a) MEDICAL COMFORTS.							
Sugar. lbs.	30	30	30	3	24	234	
Tea. "	80	30	30	4	16	106	
Cocoa. "							
Oxo. "	40	40	40	2½	10	130	
Cigarettes. "	30	30	30	2	8	98	
Bread. "							As available.
Butter. "	53	28	28	7	28	140	
Pepper. "	1	½	½	⅛	½	2½	
Salt. "	28	7	7	1	4	43	
Biscuits. "	100	50	50	25	100	300	
(b) STORES.							
Stretchers, Amb.	350	100	100	20	8	680	
Blankets.	1000	750	1000	100	400	3150	
Stretchers, Trench.				5	20	80	
Ammonia Capsules.	1000	200	200	200	800	2200	
Lamps, Acetylene, Hanging	–	–	4	2	8	12	
(c) DRESSINGS							
Shell.	600	300	300	200	800	2000	
Gauze. Plain yds	1700	1000	1000	750	3000	6700	
Wool. lbs.	100	100	100	75	300	600	
Tow. "	10	10	10	12	48	78	
Bandages. L.W. 3" No.	500	750	750	250	1000	3000	
" △ "	400	200	200	50	200	1000	
Splints, Thomas.		3	8			13	
Supports, "		3	8				
Splints, back leg with footpieces.	8	15	15	6	24	68	
Splints, arm angular.	10	10	10	6	24	60	
Splints, Listons	10	10	10	6	24	64	
" common. sets.	1	1	1	1	4	7	

APPENDIX "B" WAR DIARY VOLUME VI.   PAGE 2

138 F.A. June 1917
B.

REPORT ON OPERATIONS 7th. June - 8th. June 1917.

(1) At 6-0 p.m. on "Y" day this Field Ambulance was in position, allocated as follows :-

        H.Q.   A.D.S.   )   "A" Bearer sub-division.
)   "A" Sec. Tent sub-division.

        Collecting Post.)   "B" &"C" Sec. Bearer sub-divisions.
        VOORMEZEELE.   )   "C" Sec. Tent sub-division.

        Medical Dump.)   "B" Sec. Tent-sub-division.
        Ouderdom.   )

thus leaving 4 bearer sub-divisions in reserve.
I arranged with the Officer i/c Forward Bearers to send him 2 bearer sub-divisions of the 139th. Field Ambulance, and 2 Bearer sub-divisions of the 140th. Field Ambulance, to arrive at C.P. at Zero plus 1 hour and Zero plus 4 hours respectively, and also an additional officer, as Zero was 3-10 a.m. on the 7th. inst. These bearer sub-divisions left A.D.S. at 2;45 a.m. and 6-15 a.m. respectively and arrived at the C.P. according to schedule time.

(2) From 6-0 p.m. on the 6th. casualties continued to arrive at the A.D.S. in small numbers, and communication was maintained between the A.D.S. and the forward area. Five minutes after Zero, I decided to attempt to establish communication with the C.P. at the earliest possible moment, and a car proceeded there, and evacuation of the C.P. was carried out as quickly as the casualties arrived. About 5-30 a.m. larger numbers reached the C.P. and from 9-0 p.m. 6/6/17 to 12 noon 7th. 16 Officers, 794 O.R. and 1 German Prisoner were admitted. At 3-45 p.m. 7/6/17 the C.P. was reported clear by the Officer i/c, who requested that no more cars should be sent until required, and I then proceeded to attempt to evacuate completely the A.D.S., and 10 Cars were obtained from the Cabstand to remove lying cases to the C.M.D.S. for "Seriously wounded". These performed about 2 journeys and by about 7-0 p.m. only 30 cases in all, lying and sitting, awaited evacuation from the C.P. and A.D.S. From noon to 9-0 p.m. 7th. 24 Officers, 482 O.R. and 60 P. of W. were admitted, and casualties admitted from 9-0 p.m. to 6-0 a.m. on the 8th. totalled 10 Officers, 301 O.R. and 19 P. of W. These were nearly all evacuated by 6-0 a.m.
From 6-0 a.m. to 12 noon 8th. 112 Other Ranks and 2 P.of W. were admitted. These were all evacuated with the exception of 20 cases at 12 noon 8th.
From 12 noon until the time of relief (3-50 p.m.) 2 Officers, 238 O.R. and 5 P. of W. were admitted, making the total casualties passing through the A.D.S. 52 Officers, 1927 O.R. and 82 P. of W. At 2-50 p.m. the C.P. was handed to the 24th. Division and at 3-50 p.m. I handed over the A.D.S. to the 72nd. Field Ambulance with only 4 cases awaiting evacuation, and 6 Motor Ambulances of this Division were placed at the disposal of the Officer i/c of A.D.S. before leaving

Of the cases admitted 567 were lying cases, who were evacuated to C.M.D.S. BRANDHOEK.

3.) REMARKS.
During the whole period under view, the situation gave no cause for anxiety. With the exception of the time when assistance was asked from the cabstand, owing to 4 of the 14 cars at my disposal being temporary disabled.
Sitting cases were evacuated by Horse Ambulance and G.S. Wagons, and a large number of cases were also evacuated by motor lorries.
As communication by Motor Ambulance to the C.P. was continuous, no use was made of the trolley line from VOORMEZEELE to CAFE BELGE.

                              (continued).

Remarks (Continued).

The proportion of lying cases, seriously wounded, evacuated by this Unit, appeared to be much smaller than usual.

Casualties. (This Unit).

Casualties occurring to the personnel of this Unit, were only 2. 1 at the C.P. and a despatch rider attached to H.Q. was slightly gassed (shell) about 250 yards away from the A.D.S.

In accordance with instructions received, that the 24th. Division would relieve this Unit on the 8th. I proceeded to C.P. at about 2-0 a.m. and informed the Officer i/c Forward Bearers and the Officer i/c C.P. to make necessary arrangements.

W Ross Gardner
Lt. Col. R.A.M.C.
Commanding 138th. Field Ambulance.

9/6/17.

Vol 15

140/298

COMMITTEE FOR THE
MEDICAL HISTORY OF THE WAR
Date 10 SEP. 1917

CONFIDENTIAL.

WAR DIARY

OF

138th FIELD AMBULANCE. R.A.M.C.

FROM:- JULY 1st 1917   TO:- JULY 31st 1917.

(VOLUME VII)

Army Form C. 2118

WAR DIARY
or
INTELLIGENCE SUMMARY

VOLUME VII. PAGE I.

(Erase heading not required.)

Instructions regarding War Diaries and Intelligence Summaries are contained in F. S. Regs., Part II. and the Staff Manual respectively. Title Pages will be prepared in manuscript.

Place	Date	Hour	Summary of Events and Information	Remarks and references to Appendices
NR FLETRE Sheet 27 S.E. N 5 c 3.9	1ST		CAPT J.L.A.F LAUDER, D.S.O. M.C. R.A.M.C. reported his arrival back from leave 30/6/17. I.O.R. proceeded on leave to England from 2-12th July 1917. H.O.R. proceeded to 2nd Army Rest Camp, AMBLETEUSE. Received S.69 from A.D.M.S. (re publications to be returned in the event of Divn. moving into another Army)	WRG
"	2ND		CAPT J.L.A.F LAUDER, D.S.O. M.C. R.A.M.C. proceeded to A.D.M.S. 41st Divn. for duty during absence of A.D.M.S. on leave. I.O.R. proceeded on leave to England from 3rd - 13th July 1917.	WRG
"	3RD		Received S.621 from A.D.M.S. (Correction to Code). Received S.623 from A.D.M.S. giving map locations of Dt Units	WRG
"	4TH		CAPT. R.T. HERDMAN. R.A.M.C. reported his arrival back for duty from 72nd Bde. A.F.A.	WRG
"	6TH		Training carried out in accordance with schedule received from A.D.M.S. Establishment of "Advanced Dressing Stations" by sections. I.O.R. proceeded on leave from 7th - 17th inst.	WRG

WAR DIARY
or
INTELLIGENCE SUMMARY

(Erase heading not required.)

Army Form C. 2118

Volume VII Page II

Place	Date	Hour	Summary of Events and Information	Remarks and references to Appendices
Nr. FLETRE Sheet 27 S.E W.5 C.3 9.	7th		D.D.M.S. visited Camps. 10 R proceeded on leave from 8th – 18th inst.	WRG
"	8th		CAPT. W.M. CHESNEY, M.C. R.A.M.C. proceeded on leave to U.K. from 9th – 19th July 1917. Received S 626 from A.D.M.S. giving me location of 2nd R.F.A.	WRG
"	9th		H/Cpl. Dunn, A.B. proceeded to ENGLAND as candidate for a commission.	WRG
"	11th		Inspection of Gas Helmets & Iron Rations. Inspection of Horses by Major P.T.C. HERBERT, D.S.O. R of O. ROYAL HORSE ARTILLERY X Corps.	WRG
"	14th		Recd. O.O. No. 102 Copy No 20 from 123rd Inf. Bde. Field Ambulance & Camp inspected by Divisional Commander.	WRG

WAR DIARY or INTELLIGENCE SUMMARY

Army Form C. 2118

Volume VII Page 22

Place	Date	Hour	Summary of Events and Information	Remarks and references to Appendices
Sheet 27 SE W6 c39	15th		I.O.R. proceeded to O.C. 2nd Bde. R.F.G. H.Q. for duty in accordance with A.D.M.S. M1744 d15 F.J. Received S.636 from A.D.M.S. 41st Div. (Medical arrangements for offensive).	WW
"	17th		Capt. E.A. LUMLEY, R.A.M.C. & 40 other Ranks proceeded to Officer i/c A.D.S. Voormezeele for construction of Aid Posts (Auth. A.D.M.S. 41st Div W223 d16 F.J.). Received S.639 from A.D.M.S. 41st Div (Administrative arrangements). " S.641 from A.D.M.S. (Correction to Code). O.O. No.21 Copy No.3 received from A.D.M.S. (124th Bde. moving from area, responsibility for reception of sick from 122nd & 123rd Bde. to be on 2nd F.A.). Rec'd. O.O. No.102 from 123rd Inf. Bde.	WW
"	18th		Rec'd info in connection with operations. Inspection of Gas Helmets, Iron Rations & Steel Helmets, also of A.S.C.-H.T.	WW
"	19th		Capt. H.W. HODGSON. R.A.M.C. reported for duty	WW

Army Form C. 2118

WAR DIARY
or
INTELLIGENCE SUMMARY

VOLUME VII   PAGE IV

(Erase heading not required.)

Place	Date	Hour	Summary of Events and Information	Remarks and references to Appendices
Sheet 27SE W5c3.9.	Sept 20th		Recd. Appendices No. 24 to 00102 from 123rd Bde. I.O.R. proceeded on leave. CAPT W.M. CHESNEY, M.C. R.A.M.C. reported his arrival back from leave. Health inspection of personnel. I.O.R. forwarded to 124th Machine Gun Coy for duty in accordance with A.D.M.S. 1769. d.20th. CAPT. W.F. WILSON R.A.M.C. appointed permanent M.O. to 2/6th Royal Fusiliers & struck off the strength of this Unit. (Auth:- ADMS 41st Div. M1. d.20th).	WCG
"	21st		Attended conference of O.C's Field Ambulances at A.D.M.S Office. Inspection of personnel, Camp & Hospital by D.M.S. II Army. O.O. No 128 Copy No 15 received from 122nd Inf. Bde, also administrative instructions. Received O.O. No. 22 Copy 3 from ADMS (122nd Inf Bde. moving to Westoutre area.) Attended conference of M.O's by A.D.M.S. 41st Div. at H.Q. of this Unit.	WCG
"	22nd		Received O.O. No 23 Copy 5 from A.D.M.S 41st Div (41st Div. relieving 47th Div during nights July 24/25th & 25/26th). Transferred all cases from Hospital in accordance with above O.O.	WCG

WAR DIARY
or
INTELLIGENCE SUMMARY

Army Form C. 2118

Volume VII Page V

Place	Date	Hour	Summary of Events and Information	Remarks and references to Appendices
Sheet 27.S.E. W5 c 3.9.	23rd.		Vacated Camp at W5 c 3.9 and proceeded to YORK CAMP (WESTOUTRE AREA) Sheet 28 S.W. M3 c 25.8. & reported completion at 12.15 p.m. Received O.O. No 102 Copy 20 also Appendix III from 123rd Inf. Bde. Received S 649. 649a. & 650 from A.D.M.S. (Maps being referring to operations). O.O. No 104 Copy 17 received from 123rd Inf. Bde.	WRC
Sheet 28 S.W. M3 c 25.8.	24th.		Advance party proceeded to Divl. Rest Station (BOESCHEPE) in relief of 139th Field Ambulance in accordance with A.D.M.S. O.O. No 23. CAPT. E. A. LUMLEY & working party returned from VOORMEZEELE.	WRC
Sheet 27 S.E. R.10 a 3.3. BOESCHEPE.	25th.		Remainder of Field Ambulance proceeded to D.R.S. (Boeschepe). Relief completed by 10-30 a.m. & reported to A.D.M.S. 41st Division. H. Cars departed at 11.15 a.m. for duty at A.D.S. VOORMEZEELE in accordance with A.D.M.S. instructions.	WRC
- " -	26th.		2 Sunbeam Motor Ambulances returned from A.D.S. Voormezeele. Received S 660 from A.D.M.S. (Addition to Medical arrangements) O.O. No 105. Copy 17. received from 123rd Inf. Bde.	WRC

WAR DIARY or INTELLIGENCE SUMMARY

Army Form C. 2118

Volume VII — Page VI

Place	Date	Hour	Summary of Events and Information	Remarks and references to Appendices
Sheet 27 R10 a 3 3 BOESCHEPE	28th		2 N.C.O.'s + 33 men proceeded as working party to A.D.S. VOORMEZEELE. CAPT. L.W. BAIN. R.A.M.C. appointed permanent M.O. ½ 21st K.R.R.C. from 22nd Inst. & struck off the strength of this Units from that date. (Auth: A.D.M.S. H/51 Div. R.Q 573 d. 28/7.)	WRG
-"-	29th		Received D.O No 5 from O.C. 130th Field Ambulance.	WRG
-"-	30th	5.30 a.m.	CAPT. J.A.A.F. LAUDER. D.S.O. M.C. R.A.M.C. & CAPT. L.S.C. ROCHE. M.C. R.A.M.C. proceeded with 3 Bearer Sub-divisions (less working party at A.D.S.) to take over Forward Area, south of the Canal, with H.Q. at Collecting Post, at Shelly Dumps. CAPT. W.M. CHESNEY. M.C R.A.M.C. & CAPT H.W. HODGSON. R.A.M.C. proceeded to A.B.S. VOORMEZEELE To report to O.C. 130th Field Ambulance for duty. 3 Horse Ambulances + G.S. Wagons converted, proceeded for duty to A.D.S Voormezeele, also 3 Sunbeam & 2 Ford Cars in accordance with A.D.M.S Hst Div. S636 d. 15/7. 2. O.R. proceeded to M.D.S. LA CLYTTE (41st Div). as clerks to collect details of H/51 Div. casualties. 1 Motor Cyclist to A.D.M.S. Office for duty.	WRG

WAR DIARY or INTELLIGENCE SUMMARY

Army Form C. 2118

VOLUME VII PAGE VIII

Place	Date	Hour	Summary of Events and Information	Remarks and references to Appendices
SHEET 27 R.10.a.3.3 BOESCHEPE	3/37		STRENGTH OF UNIT:- R.A.M.C. OFFICERS 9 O.R. 193 A.S.C. H.T. OTHER RANKS 33 A.S.C. M.T. OTHER RANKS 12 CAPT. R.T. TODD. R.A.M.C. posted to this Unit from 30/7/17, & attached to 139th F.A. for temporary duty. (Auth. A.D.M.S. M.I. d. 30/7/17)	MOS

A Roe Gardner
Lt Col. R.A.M.C.
Commanding 138th Field Ambulance.

Appendix C.

2

_th. FIELD AMBULANCE OPERATION ORDER No. ___   Copy No. ___

1. The __th. Field Ambulance will relieve the Field Ambulance of the 24th. Division in the ST. ELOI (DAMMSTRASSE) sector, with H.Q. at _____. The 31st. Divl. front will be from far _____ of VOORMEZ___ to CANAL.
   Relief to be completed by 8-0 a.m. on the ___ inst.

2. Officers i/c Stations and detachments will report completion of relief or otherwise at that hour.

3. Evacuation will be carried out from 'forward' R.A.P's in DAMMSTRASSE area, to Nos. 1 & 3. original R.A.P's which will be constituted temporarily as 'Wounded Dumps', whence evacuation will be carried out by trolley or Ambulance Car to A.D.S. VOORMEZEELE. Capt. L.S.C. Roche, R.A.M.C. i/c.

4. Clearance from A.D.S. of Sick & Wounded will be direct to M.D.S. La CLYTTE Road. (M8 a.8.3.) (120th. F.A.)

5. Nominal Rolls, in duplicate, and all such other records etc., as appertain in normal Trench Warfare, will be compiled at A.D.S. e.g. A.F.W. 3118 Field Medical Card & Kit Labels. (No Pack-store book will be kept.)
   Nominal Roll of all patients sent to M.D.S. will accompany, the duplicate copy of which will, however be retained at A.D.S.

6. DISPOSITION.

Sub-div.		Med. Dump.	A.D.S.	R.A.P's Nos. 1 & 3.	Forwd. R.A.P's
"A" Sec.	B.			⊕	
	T.				
"B" Sec.	B.				
	T.				
"C" Sec.	B.	✶			
	T.				

   ⊕ Parties from this sub-division will also occupy Nos. 2 & 4 original R.A.P's and establish posts at (Sheet 28 S.W. E.) O.2.c.2.7. and O.2.c.3.3. (DAMMSTRASSE) and reinforce "B" Section bearer sub-division.
   ✶ This sub-division will be held in reserve for the 'forward' area, or as a relief for "__" Section bearer sub-division.

7. Advanced parties from the sub-divisions that will eventually take over, and as above shewn, will proceed to A.D.S., Collecting Posts & 'Forward' area, to work with 24th. Division preparatory to taking over. (Ref. paras Nos. 1 & 6.)

8. Responsibility for evacuations from new R.A.P's to A.D.S. and control of such Ambulances as proceed beyond the latter station, will rest with Officer i/c 'Forward' area.

9. Capt. E. A. LUMLEY, R.A.M.C. will be Officer i/c 'Forward' area, with H.Q. at VOORMEZEELE C.P. or Nos. 1 or 3. original R.A.P's and he will report which of these sites has been decided on by him.

10. Resting of Bearer sub-divisions will be at VOORMEZEELE until Officer i/c Forward area shall desire otherwise, thereafter at OUDERDOM. Reliefs will be carried out as far as possible at dusk and dawn.

11. 'A.D.S. Limber' and water cart ("A" Section) will proceed to A.D.S. Mule team of the Limber will return to OUDERDOM, that of the water cart will remain at VOORMEZEELE. This water cart will be controlled by Officer i/c 'Forward area', who will dispose it as he thinks fit. Similarly he will arrange hours of refilling, with Officer i/c Ouder-

/12.

12. MOTOR AMBULANCES. 1 Ford Car will be stationed at A.D.S. and under orders of Officer i/c 'Forward' area. This car, may, however be employed by A.D.S. under arrangements with Capt. E.A. LUMLEY. Motor Ambulance park will be at OUDERDOM.

13. Ouderdom station will be held as Medical Dump and for care of Local sick, Capt. W.M. CHESNEY, R.A.M.C. i/c.

14. Officer i/c Forward area will arrange to occupy with a minimum staff Nos. 3 & 4 original R.A.P's and 1 trolley truck will be attached to each of these posts. All other trucks (R.A.M.C. 80) will be allocated as he considers necessary. He will also occupy the DAMSTRASSE Posts. This Officer will be responsible for the evacuation by trolley, insofar as that occurs in connection with clearance from 'forward' area (new DAMSTRASSE area) R.A.P's and similarly with transfer of Medical Stores etc., forward of A.D.S.

15. A C K N O W L E D G E.

11/6/17.

Issued at 4-0 p.m.

W Ross Gardner
Lt. Col. R.A.M.C.
Commanding 138th. Field Ambulance.

Copy No. 1. File.
2. & 3. War Diary.
4. A.D.M.S.
5. F.A. of the 24th. Division.
6-8. Officers i/c Stations.
9-10. Spare.

Appendix 2

SECRET.

138th. FIELD AMBULANCE OPERATION ORDER NO:6.   COPY..No.2...........

1. The following will be the scheme of evacuation, which will hold in the event of this Field Ambulance having to make special arrangements for dealing with sudden and considerable casualties in the Northern portion of this Divisional Front. (from North of ROSEWOOD to CANAL).

   It should be understood that these arrangements constitute but a specialised portion of the general scheme for the evacuation of wounded, at present in force, and that although administered distinctly, should be co-ordinated to a reaction elsewhere and vice versa.

2. EVACUATION - STRETCHER CASES.

   (a) Will be conveyed by trolley from WHITE CHATEAU to COLLECTING POST at SPOIL BANK. They will be transferred there, by Ford Cars, & conveyed to Advanced Motor Ambulance Park (D 32. central) re-transferred to Sunbeam Cars, and thence to VOORMEZEELE and A.D.S. The route taken by Motor Ambulances, will be overland track, which extends from SPOIL BANK to I 31.a.8.8. and then by that portion of the VOORMEZEELE - YPRES ROAD which extends from that point (I 31.a.8.8.) to VOORMEZEELE VILLAGE.
   Should he consider it advisable, Officer i/c 'Forward' area (Capt. J.La. F. LAUDER, R.A.M.C.) may run Sunbeam Cars as far as SPOIL BANK, and thereby dispense with the intermediate transfer from Ford to Sunbeam Car at I. 32 central.
   A second Motor Ambulance Park will be at VOORMEZEELE, and as soon as an Ambulance arrives at A.D.S. another will proceed up to I32 central (Advanced Motor Ambulance Park)

   (b) WALKING WOUNDED.
   Walking cases will proceed from R.A.P. (White Chateau) down cart track, which extends from original R.A.P. No. 1. (I 32.d.1.3.) past ARUNDEL, UPPER & LOWER OOSTHOEK FARMS to O. 3.b.4.8. and then bifurcates its two branches proceeding to O. 4.d.4.2. and O.3.d.7.7.
   Both these tracks, as well as the overland track mentioned in

   para (2) (a) already dilineated by whitened posts, will be still further indicated by directing flags or signboards. Walking

   cases will proceed from this Collecting Post by overland to A.D.S. or be conveyed there, if such can be arranged, by G.S. wagons converted.
   In the event of the tracks becoming impassable to wheeled traffic, from wet weather, the following viae of evacuation will hold :-
   (A) by use of VOORMEZEELE - ST: ELOI - YPRES ROAD.
   (B) by trolley direct to VOORMEZEELE.

3. Owing to the inadequate accommodation possibly at new R.A.P's the Collecting Posts at SPOIL BANK and original R.A.P No.1. should be prepared to assume, if necessary the duties of subsidiary R.A.P's as regards the care of, as well as the disposal of wounded.

4. WATER. Spoil Bank is provided with an adequate water supply, in the shape of tanks.

5. EQUIPMENT - BEARERS.

   Skeleton equipment only, will be worn. Valise and Greatcoat to be left at H.Q.

/ 6 (DISPOSITION)

6. DISPOSITION.

		A.D.S. No. D. Sp.Bank. No. 2. Orig.RAP.		C.P's		F. Brs. Trolley teams.		D 32 central. Ad. Motor Amb. Park.
		Off.	O.R	Off.	O.R.	Off.	O.R.	O.R.
Off.	O.R.							
	9							*(Unloading & Loading parties)
2	12							*(Distributed between Posts No 1 & 2.)
	9							*(No.1. Post)
1	37							*(Stationed at No. 2 Post. In reserve Bearer sub-div "A" Sect.)
1	37							*("b" Sec. B sub-div)
	9							*(Loading & unloading)

TRANSPORT.

"A" Sect. "A.D.S. LIMBER" ————* Mule teams will return to H.Q.
"B" "   "   "   ————*

MOTOR AMBULANCES.

Sunbeam. Ford.
  3 ———— 2 ———————*(In reserve as main Amb. Park)
        1 ———————————————*(No.1 Spoil Bank) C.P.)

7. A C K N O W L E D G E.

W Ross Gardner
Lt. Col. R.A.M.C.
Commanding 138th. Field Ambulance.

13th. June 1917.

Issued at 3-0 p.m.

Copy No.1 File.
     2 & 3. War Diary.
     4. A.D.M.S.
     5. O i/c Forward bearers.
     6. Spare (Officers)
     7-10 Spare.

SECRET.

APPENDIX "E".

Report on operations of the 14th., inst.

(1) At 4-0 p.m. on the 14th, inst this Field Ambulance was in position as follows :-

    2 Bearer sub-divisions for the 124th., Bde. on the right.
    2 Bearer sub-Divisions for the 122nd., Bde. on the left.
    1 Tent sub-division at A.D.S. VOORMEZEELE.
    1 Tent sub-division between aid-posts Nos. 1 - 4.
    1 Tent sub-division remained at H.Q.

(2) CASUALTIES.

Casualties arrived at the A.D.S. in small numbers about 9-0 p.m. and continued to do so until about 1-0 a.m.
Cases from WHITE CHATEAU were evacuated to A.D.S. as quickly as they arrived, there being no congestion at any time.
From 9-0 p.m. 3 Officers, 118 Other Ranks and 8 Prisoners of War were admitted, and from 6-0 a.m. 15th. to 8-30 a.m. 1 Officer 34 Other Ranks were admitted, making the total number of casualties passing through A.D.S. Officers 4. Other Ranks 152 and P. of W. 8
At 7-30 a.m. 15th. there were no cases awaiting evacuation at the A.D.S.
Of the 164 cases admitted, 42 were lying cases.

(3) EVACUATIONS.

All lying cases were evacuated in Motor Ambulances, and sitting cases in Horse Ambulances and G.S. Wagons, converted.

(4) REMARKS.

During the period mentioned above, there was no cause for anxiety at any time, evacuations being carried out very smoothly. There were no casualties to R.A.M.C. personnel after Zero hour.

15/6/17.

                                        Lt. Col. R.A.M.C.
                         Commanding 138th. Field Ambulance.

Appendix 7.

138th. FIELD AMBULANCE OPERATION ORDER NO. 7.   COPY NO. 2

1. The 138th. Field Ambulance will be relieved in the line by a Field Ambulance of the 17th., Division. Relief to be completed by 3.0 a.m. on the 28th. June.

2. Officers i/c of detachments will report completion of the relief or otherwise at that hour.

3. The Officer i/c A.D.S. and 'Forward' area will hand over the A.D.S. Spoil Bank C.P. and the 'Original' R.A.P's No. 1 & 3 to the incoming Unit, and will fully explain to the relieving Officer, all details of the present scheme of evacuation of 41st., Divisional casualties.

4. He will arrange that only half of the personnel of this Unit is relieved at one time, in order that the relieving party may become thoroughly acquainted with the ground.

5. On completion of relief, he will proceed with the personnel and transport of this Unit, and report at this H.Q. (N.1. d. 2.2.).

6. On completion of relief the bearer sub-division and transport of the 140th. Field Ambulance will be instructed by the Officer i/c A.D.S. to report at this H.Q.

7. STORES.
The Lieut. Quartermaster will arrange to hand over all stores, arms, red cross and ordnance, in excess of War Establishment, to the incoming Unit. Receipts in triplicate will be obtained, and 2 Copies of each will be handed in to this Office.
He will arrange for 2 G.S. Wagons to report to the Officer i/c A.D.S. by 8-30 a.m. 28th. June.

8. This Field Ambulance, when relieved, will proceed to the Rest Billets at R. 34. c.4.1. at present occupied by the 69th. Field Ambulance, 23rd., Division.

9. March route will be as follows :-
LA CLYTTE - LOCRE - THE ASYLUM, BAILLEUL, thence by side track to ST. JANS CAPPEL ROAD, then via ST. JANS CAPPEL & SCHAEXKEN to R 4. a.7.3., thence to R. 34. c.4.1.

10. A C K N O W L E D G E.

W Ross Gardner
Lt. Col. R.A.M.C.
Commanding 138th. Field Ambulance.

26/6/17.
Issued at 7.30. p.m.
Copy No. 1 Fths.
       2 & 3. War Diary.
       4. A.D.M.S. 41st. Division.
       5.
       6. O.C. th. Field Ambce's.
       7. Officer i/c A.D.S. & Forward area.
       8. In Spare.

Confidential

War Diary

of the

138th Field Ambulance.

From August 1st 1917 till August 31st 1917.

(Volume VIII)

COMMITTEE FOR THE
MEDICAL HISTORY OF THE WAR
Date — 5 NOV. 1917

Army Form C. 2118

WAR DIARY
or
INTELLIGENCE SUMMARY
(Erase heading not required.)

VOLUME VII PAGE 1

AUGUST 1917

Place	Date	Hour	Summary of Events and Information	Remarks and references to Appendices
BOESCHEPE. SHEET 27 S.E. R 10 a 3.3	1st.		CAPT. R.T. TODD. R.A.M.C. posted to this Unit from 30th July, and attached to 139th Field Ambulance for temporary duty. LIEUT. R.D. PASSEY. R.A.M.C. posted to this Unit from 31st July, and attached to 139th Field Ambulance for temporary duty. 2 Reinforcements A.S.C.H.T. arrived for duty. 1 O.R. killed in action. Casualties admitted to this Divl. Rest Station from noon 31/July to noon 1st Aug. Wounded 43. Sick 62.	W.D.
"	2d.		A.D.M.S. 41st Divn. held Medical Board at this Divl. Rest Station. Received S.687 from A.D.M.S. (Battle Traffic Circuits). Medical & Sanitary Care of H.Q. & 3rd Mob. Lab. Coy. arranged during absence of M.O. i/c. (C. Duns. 1832 a 2 f17) Casualties admitted from noon 1st - noon 2nd Aug. Wounded 153. Sick 52	W.D.
"	3d.		Received S.665 from A.D.M.S. (Names of Farms East of Old British Line South of HOLLEBEKE). Casualties admitted from noon 2 - 3rd Aug. Wounded 15 Sick 164.	W.D.
"	4th		CAPT. R.T. TODD. R.A.M.C. reported his arrival for duty from 139th Field Ambulance. 2 O.R.s. A.S.C.-H.T. transferred to R.G.A & proceeded to Base Depot. Casualties admitted from noon 3rd - 4th Aug. Wounded 12 Sick 244.	W.D.

WAR DIARY or INTELLIGENCE SUMMARY

Army Form C. 2118

Volume VIII   Page IV

Place	Date	Hour	Summary of Events and Information	Remarks and references to Appendices
BOESCHEPE SHEET 27SE R.10.a.3.3.	5th		2 O.R's. arrived as reinforcements to A.S.C.-M.T. attached. 1 O.R. M.T.-A.S.C. of this unit died of wounds. Casualties admitted from noon 4-5th Aug.	WCG
"	6th		5 Riders sent to 3rd Army Remount Section in accordance with A.D.M.S. instructions 1826 of 1/8/17 & struck off the strength of this unit. 1 O.R. R.A.M.C. Died from Gas Poisoning. Casualties admitted from noon 5-6th Aug. Wounded 17 Incl.17H.	WCG
"	7th		Capt. E.A. Lumley, R.A.M.C. proceeded to "Forward Area" in relief of Capt. L.S.C. Roche. M.C. R.A.M.C. who reported to H.Q. for duty. 1 Ford & 2 Sunbeam Ambulance Cars returned from 139th F.A. for duty at this unit.	WCG
"	8th		D.M.S. 2nd Army. D.D.M.S. I.K. Corps. & A.D.M.S. 41st Div. visited Camp. & inspected hospital camp arrangements &c. Received S.693 from A.D.M.S. (Corrections to Codes)	WCG
"	9th		A.D.M.S. 41st Div. held Medical Board at this D.R.S. Capt. J.L.A.F. Lauder, D.S.O. M.C. R.A.M.C. reported his arrival from "Forward Area" on being relieved by Capt. E.A. Lumley, R.A.M.C. (Authority A.D.M.S. 41st Div. 1888 of 8/7/17) 1 O.R. R.A.M.C. Killed in action.	WCG

WAR DIARY
or
INTELLIGENCE SUMMARY
(Erase heading not required.)

Army Form C. 2118

VOLUME VIII
PAGE III

Place	Date	Hour	Summary of Events and Information	Remarks and references to Appendices
BUESCHEPE SHEET 27 S.E. R.10 a 3 3	10th		Received S.697 from A.D.M.S 41st Div (Correct to B.A.B. French Code)	WRG
—	11th		Attended conference of O.C's Field Ambulances at A.D.M.S. 41st Div at 11.0 a.m. Horse Transport returned from 139th Field Ambulance.	WRG
—	12th		20 O.R's R.A.M.C. returned from "Forward Area". CAPT. J.E. & F LAUDER D.S.O. M.C. R.A.M.C. proceeded to A.D.M.S. 41st Div for duty. 36 Other ranks from R.R.'s proceeded to 2nd Army Rest Camp, AMBLETEUSE. 10 R.A.M.C. arrived as reinforcements to this Unit. Received O.O No.24 from A.D.M.S & O.O./132 & 133 from 122nd Inf. Bde. (& rely) Received instructions from A.D.M.S re Medical care of 124th Bde. Necessary arrangements made.	WRG
—	13th		CAPT. L.S.C. ROCHE. M.C. R.A.M.C. proceeded on leave to England from 13th - 23rd Aug.	WRG

WAR DIARY or INTELLIGENCE SUMMARY

Army Form C. 2118

VOLUME VIII PAGE IV

Place	Date	Hour	Summary of Events and Information	Remarks and references to Appendices
BOESCHEPE SHEET 27SE R10 a 3 3	14th		CAPT. E.A. LUMLEY, R.A.M.C. and remainder of Bearer Sub-divisions returned from Forward Area. Received S.700 from A.D.M.S. (Forecast of disposition of Bnt Units for 16th).	WRG
"	15th		LIEUT. R.D. PASSEY. R.A.M.C. granted leave to England from 15-25th August. CAPT. W.M. CHESNEY, M.C. R.A.M.C. reported his arrival back for duty from "Forward Area". CAPT. R.T. HERDMAN. R.A.M.C. reported his arrival back from 12th EAST SURREY Regt. for duty.	WRG
"	16th		CAPT. H.W. HODGSON, R.A.M.C. proceeded as temporary M.O. i/c 41st Div. Train A.S.C. during absence of CAPT. J.J. REYNOLDS, R.A.M.C., in accordance with A.D.M.S. instructions. 7 R.A.M.C. reinforcements posted to this Unit.	WRG
"	17th		Received S.702 from A.D.M.S. (Locations of Units in Rest Area). Military Medals awarded to 2 O.R. of this Unit for gallantry on 1/6/17.	WRG

Army Form C. 2118

WAR DIARY
or
INTELLIGENCE SUMMARY

VOLUME VIII   PAGE V

(Erase heading not required.)

Place	Date	Hour	Summary of Events and Information	Remarks and references to Appendices
BOESCHEPE SHEET 27SE R.10 a 3.3.	18TH		CAPT. R.T. HERDMAN. R.A.M.C. proceeded to D.D.M.S. X Corps for duty as temporary M.O. i/c X Corps Troops. 2n Bar to M.M. awarded to 1 O.R. of this Unit & M.M. to 1 other Rank for gallantry in the Field on 3/4/17 & 1/5/17 respectively.	WD
"	20TH		Received S703 from A.D.M.S. (Maps of new Divl. Area)	WD
"	24TH		Received O.O. No. 27. from A.D.M.S. 46th Div. regarding move from D.R.S. holding party consisting of 2 Officers & 1 section only to remain. Received O.O. No. 129 from 124 Inf. Bde. regarding area to which Bde. would proceed. also March table. CAPT. L.S.C. ROCHE. M.C. R.A.M.C. proceeded to D.D.M.S. HAVRE. for duty as Mental Attendant in accordance with A.D.M.S. instructions M.2009 of 23/7/17.	WD
"	25th	6.0a.m.	4 Officers & 2 sections with transport vacated D.R.S. and proceeded to STAPLE area & billeted for the night. 1 Section, Capt. W.M. CHESNEY. M.C. R.A.M.C. i/c & CAPT. R.T. TODD remained at D.R.S. as holding party.	WD

Army Form C. 2118

WAR DIARY
or
INTELLIGENCE SUMMARY

Volume VIII Page VI

(Erase heading not required.)

Instructions regarding War Diaries and Intelligence Summaries are contained in F.S. Regs. Part II. and the Staff Manual respectively. Title Pages will be prepared in manuscript.

Place	Date	Hour	Summary of Events and Information	Remarks and references to Appendices
STAPLE AREA	26th	6:30am	Proceeded by March Route to CORMETTE (Sheet 27A S.E. Q 34 a 5.5) in accordance with March table 124th Inf. Bde. & prepared Camp for reception of patients in accordance with ADMS O.O. 27.	MCS
CORMETTE Sheet 27A Q 34 a 5.5	27th		A.D.M.S. 41st Division visited Camp. Capt. J. la F. LAUDER, D.S.O. M.C. R.A.M.C. reported his arrival back from ADMS 41st Div. for duty. LIEUT. R.D. PASSEY, R.A.M.C. granted 2 days extension of leave to 27K.	MCS
"	28th		LIEUT. R.D. PASSEY, R.A.M.C. reported his arrival back from leave. Received Secret G.70 from 41st Div H.Q. (List of Brit Code names).	MCS
"	31st		LIEUT-COL. W. ROSS GARDNER, R.A.M.C. granted leave from 31st Aug - 10th SEPT 1917, to proceed to England. 124th Infantry Bde. inspected by Commander-in-Chief at 11.0 a.m. at H.Q.rs of 21st K.R.R. Corps.	MCS

31/8/17.

V. Anderson Capt. R.A.M.C.
for O.C. 138th Field Ambulance.

CONFIDENTIAL.

WAR DIARY
OF
138th FIELD AMBULANCE.

SEPTEMBER 1st, 1917 — SEPTEMBER 30th, 1917.

(VOLUME IX)

Army Form C. 2118

WAR DIARY
or
INTELLIGENCE SUMMARY
(Erase heading not required.)

Vol. 9

PAGE 1

Place	Date	Hour	Summary of Events and Information	Remarks and references to Appendices
CORMETTE S1427A S.E. Q34 a 5.5.	1.9.17		Weather fine. Attempted conference w/ O.C.'s Ambul. conference through O/C next place.	[illegible]
do	2.9.17		Sgt. Ansell Lecture Bearers. S. 7/41 (weather & wind) received	[illegible]
do	3/9/17		Nothing of note	[illegible]
do	4.9.17		Weather v. poor. Bearers (work to improve)	[illegible]
do	5.9.17		Weather poor. Recvd S. 7/4 (correction to B.R.S. Cory) & 7th hosp. (Shrewsbury frees.) Rams D/m 15 bearers today. Pay to moves to Rouy. Camp w/ Lieut Astill	[illegible]
do	6.9.17		Weather continuous Rain. Training heavy dislocation	[illegible]
do	7.9.17		Weather bright. 2100 Passy Rave. Appendix to Nr 1e (Personnel) 15 k.n.r.c.	[illegible]

WAR DIARY
or
INTELLIGENCE SUMMARY

Army Form C. 2118

Vol. IX PAGE 11

Place	Date	Hour	Summary of Events and Information	Remarks and references to Appendices
Connected [?] 93rd A.S.S Sheet 27A SE	4.9.17	17	Weather Rack near & Col. to proceed to 185th Fd. Ambulance for Ridge compl.	WBS
do	5.9.17	17	Weather fair & warm. 11 OR proceeded from Hospital to 2nd Army Rest Camp.	WBS
do	6.9.17	17	Weather dull & cloudy. Dull. Lt. R.A. Horner DSMDE Evacd. for half. Received News To No. 28 (21.Hmm 188th Fd. Amb / section)	WBS
do	10.9.17	17	Capt. W.A. Hosson RAMC proceeds to England to expert at Training Cntr Black Pool for duty in accordance with A.O. 205 & 1st Div. M 2130 & 9-9-17	WBS
do	11.9.17	17	Lt. Col. W. Roo Gordon RAMC reported his arrival back from leave. Received S 722 from ADMS 4.1st Div. (Gas shell Bombardments)	WBS
do	12.9.17	17	Weather fine. Received G 557/33/5 from 21st Div H.Q. S 726 from ADMS	WBS

Army Form C. 2118

WAR DIARY
or
INTELLIGENCE SUMMARY
(Erase heading not required.)

Vol. IX PAGE 111

Place	Date	Hour	Summary of Events and Information	Remarks and references to Appendices
CORAMITTE/2 Q 34 a 5.5 Sheet 27 A.S.E	9/17		Received O.O. N° 30 Copy N° 3 from A.D.M.S. (41st Div.) concentration in forward area	WRS
do 13	9/17		Weather fine. Rough and stormy during night. Received Secret R 732 pm 124 Bde H.Q. (Billeting Parties) 4.0. 131 Copy No 7 (Move of Bde) Sent g 625 pm 41st Div H.Q. (Cancellation of code cells) A.O. 130 Copy No 14 from 124 Bde H.Q. " Secret R 749 pm 124 Bde H.Q. (Lorries for Baggage) evacuates all patients from Hospital Estues to C.C.S, B.R.S. on duty and struck Hospital Camp at 3.0 P.M. Cases arriving after evacuated to S. All being C.C.S cases and was unable do such	WRS

WAR DIARY
or
INTELLIGENCE SUMMARY
(Erase heading not required.)

Army Form C. 2118

Vol. IX PAGE IV

Place	Date	Hour	Summary of Events and Information	Remarks and references to Appendices
14 WALLON CAPPEL AREA Sheet 27.0.30.b.7.5.	9	19	Vacated camp at 7.0 a.m. and proceeded in accordance with 124? Bde. O.O. No 131. to Wallon Cappel area, arriving at 2.45 p.m. Map reference of Camp. Sheet 27 O 30 b 75 (N. of Ste MARIE CAPPEL) Received S 731 from a.D.m.S. 41st Div (Cancellation of Code Calls) " Secret R 753 from 124 Bde. HQ. (Further Administrative Instructions)	W̶P̶G̶
15 BOESCHEPE Sheet 27 S.E. R 10 a 3.3.	9	17	Received at Sheet 27 O 30 b 75 at 1.0 P.M. and proceeded to BOESCHEPE (41st D.R.S.) in accordance with 124 Bde O.O. No 132, arriving at 6.15 P.M. (Sheet 27 S.E. R 10 a 3. 3.) Reported location of Unit to A.D.m.S 41st Div and Bde HQ. Car sent out at 6.30 P.M. to all units of Bde for collection of sick for admission to Hospital Location of D.R.S. Sheet 29 S.E. R 10 a 3 3	W̶P̶G̶

WAR DIARY or INTELLIGENCE SUMMARY

Army Form C. 2118

VOL. IX PAGE V

Place	Date	Hour	Summary of Events and Information	Remarks and references to Appendices
BOESCHEPE R.10.a.3.3 Sheet 27.S.E.	15.9.17		Received S.732 from ADMS. (Further Administrative Instructions) " O.O.132 from 124 Bde (Continuation of Bde march)	MGS
"	16.9.17		Weather fine. Received K.781 from 124 Bde (Amendment to instructions) " K.782 " " (Amended instructions re Ammunition) " K.783 " " " S.739 from ADMS (Amended instructions) ADMS 41st Div. visited Camp.	MGS
"	17.9.17		Received S.740 from ADMS 41st Div (Additional instructions) " S.743 " " (Location of units) " S.744 " " (Maps) " S.166 from O.C. 139 C.F.O. Lt. Col. W. Ross Gartrue Ramc attended conference at ADMS office at 3.0 P.M. Received K.810 from 124 Bde (Amended instructions)	MGS

WAR DIARY or INTELLIGENCE SUMMARY

Army Form C. 2118

Vol. IX PAGE VI

Place	Date	Hour	Summary of Events and Information	Remarks and references to Appendices
BOESCHEPE R.10.a.3.3 Sht 27 S.E.	18-9-17		Received S.746 (Withdrawal of Working Party) S.748 (Amendments and additions – medical arrangements) from ADMS 41st Div. Also received from ADMS 21st Div. S.757, S.752 (1st sketches for 140th & 2d S.753 (Mules for trollies). S.762 (Enquiry re Capt Rudd, Staff Capt 2d A. S.757 (Code correction) and S.757 (Casualty book evacuation to C.C.S. 5 sided platforms and 50 Thomas splints & suspension bars sent by G.S. Wagon. 6.140.2.0. Working party carried out & two S.R.S. by returning wagons. Weather good. Rain during night 2 men reported for duty as Water Wardens at R.2.C.6.6 in relief of R.A.M.C. personnel.	kRG
do	19-9-17		Received R.828 from 12th Bde (Substitutions and additions instructions) S.732 " ADMS 41st Div (Further administrative instructions) S.762 " (Instructions for Gas Sentries)	WRG

Army Form C. 2118

WAR DIARY
or
INTELLIGENCE SUMMARY
(Erase heading not required.)

Vol IX   PAGE VIII

Instructions regarding War Diaries and Intelligence Summaries are contained in F. S. Regs., Part II. and the Staff Manual respectively. Title Pages will be prepared in manuscript.

Place	Date	Hour	Summary of Events and Information	Remarks and references to Appendices
BOESCHEPE R 10 A 3.3 Sht 27 SE	23-9-17		Received O.O. No 32 (Relief of 9th by 21st Div at D.R.S) and S770 (Honr of Div) from ADMS 41st Div. All personnel and transport returned to HQ Boeschepe from 140 F.A. Received S(W 520) from ADMS. " S 768 (Amendment to O.O. 31.) (Casualties Personnel during Operations: Officers wounded 2. O.R. wounded 21.)	WR5
"	24-9-17		1 O.R. M.T. A.S.C. died of wounds. Weather very wet. All 41st Div cars transferred later to CCS or duty in accordance with ADMS instructions. Received O.O. No 33 from ADMS. 1 Officer 018.O.R.S arrived as advance party from 65th F.A.	WR5
"	25-9-17		CAPT. E.A. LUMLEY, R.A.M.C. evacuated to C.C.S. (Shell contusion knee) Lt Col W. Roofarden R.A.M.C attended conference at ADm.S Office at 10 A.M.	

WAR DIARY
or
INTELLIGENCE SUMMARY
(Erase heading not required.)

Army Form C. 2118

VOL. IX   PAGE VII

Place	Date	Hour	Summary of Events and Information	Remarks and references to Appendices
BOESCHEPE R 10 a 3 3 Sht 27 S.E	19-9-17		3 Bearer Sub divisions Transport etc proceeded at 10·30 A.M. to report to O.C. 140 F.A. in accordance with A.D.M.S. S 724 d 11/9/17. (Capt W. M. Chesney, 'C' 'B' & 'E') (Capt E.A. Dumby, 'C' 'A' Section) (Capt J.L. & Landir, Capt R.T. Ford and Lt D.A. Morris U.S.M.O. R.C.) + Lunch Wood)	MCB
do	20-9-17		Weather stormy during early morning. 30 O.R's from D.R.S. proceeded to 2nd Army Rest Camp in accordance with A.D.M.S. W 1620 d 19 9/17. Received from A.D.M.S. 41st Div. S 757 (Locations) CAPT. W.M. CHESNEY. M.C. R.A.M.C. evacuated to C.C.S. suffering from G.S.W. Chin.	MCB
do	21-9-17		Weather fine. Received from A.D.M.S. 41st Div. S 765.	MCB
"	22-9-17		Received from A.D.M.S. O.O. No 31. (Relief of Div. by 39th Div.)	MCB

WAR DIARY
or
INTELLIGENCE SUMMARY

Army Form C. 2118

Vol. IX PAGE 14

Place	Date	Hour	Summary of Events and Information	Remarks and references to Appendices
BOESCHEPE R 10 a 3.3. Sheet 27 SE	25-9-17		Received S.771 from ADMS and S.C.G. 750 from 122 Bde. Remainder of 66 ? a. arrived. D.R.S. and Camp handed over at 12 noon. 30 patients at handed over. Weather very hot.	WD
"	26-9-17		Inspection of Gas Helmets, Iron Rations and Steel Helmets held. Received from 122 Bde 0.0.14.6. Horse transport proceeded by march route at 12 noon for WORMHOUDT & remained overnight prior to proceeding to LEFFRINCKHOUCKE.	WD
LEFFRINCK- HOUCKE C 5 a 5.5 Sheet 19	27-9-17		Weather fine. Rain during early morning. Received S.C.G. 759 (Embarking instructions) Vacated Camp at Boeschepe and marched to Steenvoorde where personnel entrained for Teteghem thence detraining took place. F.A. Men marched to LEFFRINCKHOUCKE in accordance with S.C.G. 773/122 Bde. Horse transport proceeded from WORMHOUDT and arrived at LEFFRINCKHOUCKE at 3.0 P.M.	WD

WAR DIARY
or
INTELLIGENCE SUMMARY

(Erase heading not required.)

Army Form C. 2118

Vol. IX PAGE I

Place	Date	Hour	Summary of Events and Information	Remarks and references to Appendices
LA PANNE, Sheet XI W.20.c.7.9.	28-9-17		Vacated Camp at LEFFRINCKHOUCKE and proceeded by march route to LA PANNE. Reported arrival of F.A. at 12 noon at ADMS. 1ode H.Q. and made necessary arrangements for collection of sick. LT. D.A. HORNER. U.S.M.O.R.C. proceed. to 19.1 Middlesex Regt. as temporary M.O./C. that unit during absence of Capt. NASH R.A.M.C. on leave. Weather very hot.	WG
LA PANNE.	29-9-17		ADMS. 41st Div. visited Hospital and Camp. LT & Q.M. J. DODDS. R.A.M.C. and 5 O.R's proceeded on leave to England from 30-9-17 to 10-10-17. Weather very hot.	WG
LA PANNE.	30-9-17		Lt. Col. W. Roo Farrar attended conference of O.C.s of F.A.s of 41 Div. at Office of ADMS. at 10 A.M.	WG

MacGrasinParn
Lt. Col. R.A.M.C.
O.C. 138
1/2 F.a. Ambulance

(CONFIDENTIAL.)

WAR DIARY

OF

138TH FIELD AMBULANCE.

From :- October 1st 1917. To :- October 31st 1917.

(VOLUME X).

COMMITTEE FOR THE
MEDICAL HISTORY OF THE WAR

Date -8 DEC. 1917

WAR DIARY

INTELLIGENCE SUMMARY

Army Form C. 2118

Volume X, Page I

138th Field Ambulance

Place	Date	Hour	Summary of Events and Information	Remarks and references to Appendices
LA PANNE West 7.6. Sheet 11 SE	1-10-17		Capt R.T. TODD R.A.M.C. (T.C.) hostels as temporary Medical Officer in charge. 15th Adm. 6. Regt. vice Capt. Macfadden invalided sick. Weather – very bright & hot. Received S 776 from A.D.M.S. (Supply communication with Boundaries). 6. O.R's. proceeded on leave from 3/10/17 to 17/10/17. 19 cases admitted and 17 transferred to Corps Rest Station	MCS
LA PANNE	2-10-17		Weather – Bright & hot. Received S 2287 from A.D.M.S. (Re. David Lloyd) Baths Marquee at XV Corps Reinforcement Camp.) Bathing parades daily at 3 p.m. 15 cases admitted & returned to duty.	MCS
LA PANNE	3-10-17		Weather dull all morning, brighter in afternoon. A.D.M.S. HIOTLON inspected R.A.M.C. Personnel, A.S.C. M.T. A.S.C. M.T. Personal Equipment, Camp, Camp arrangements & Hospital for Helmets. Steel Helmets & Gas Rations inspected. 22 Reinforcements arrived from 14 Base details & taken on the strength & accordingly. Received S.M.P.S. from A.D.M.S. (Master) and S 1510. Return new type Army Form A. Ltd.	MCS
LA PANNE	4-10-17		Weather – bright & warm. Received S 777 from A.D.M.S. (encoder to Corps BAB 3) 6 OR proceeded on leave from 5/10/17 to 15/10/17. Received W.O. 34 from A.D.M.S. re relief of 1/8 "East Lancs" Field Ambulance by the unit in the NIEPORT BAINS COAST "DUNKERQUE" & DUNKERQUE BAINS	MCS

WAR DIARY / INTELLIGENCE SUMMARY

Army Form C. 2118

138th (H) Bty RFA Vol. X Page II

Place	Date	Hour	Summary of Events and Information	Remarks and references to Appendices
LA PANNE	4-10-17		Received Warning Order Batty No 9 from 122nd Inf Bde. 1 R.A.M.C. reinforcement arrived. Sent 1/2 Sect Para Ambulance at OOST-DUNKERKE BAINS. NIEPORT BAINS – OOST DUNKERKE road preparatory to taking over.	W2Q
LA PANNE	5-10-17		Capt L.S. ROCHE RAMC 1/c 'C' Section proceeded to OOST-DUNKERKE. Brought X 4 C 75 80 milk. on ADS Rouka or into Sect. e. 1 Motor Ambulance. Car in advance party. Established over from 1/2 Sect Para g Amb. Capt R.T. HERDMAN RAMC 1/c 'B' Section proceeded to OOST-DUNKERKE BAINS (HRe F.A.) R 27 e 55 70. (to advance park to road over NIEPORT BAINS - f MB 14 10 4.2) and LAITERIE ROYALE (R29 e7055) with 1 ADS lender, water cart and Motor Ambulance.	W2Q
LA PANNE	6-10-17		Weather showed much colder at Dr. HOWARD is more reported at 9/am for temporary duty from 139th F.A. Received S 779 from A/OM A/C Section. Provided with Capt T. H. 'F LAUDER 1/c Medical H Pers. 9ft & her & transport to OOST-DUNKERKE BAINS relieved. Relief completed by 6 pm in Capt R T HERDMAN RAMC proceeded to 41st Divisional Army unit 1 Nursing Orderly & 1 servant as an M o/c in residence with THOMAS. Received Medical Arrangements as O.O. 34. from A/OM S 41st Div Carty 8TH hrs returns return transit a 75 the Caps Real Stables & 1 b.c.c.	W2Q

OOST-DUNKERKE BAINS R 27 c 55 80 Sheet 7A

WAR DIARY
INTELLIGENCE SUMMARY

13 BFA Field Ambulance

Army Form C. 2118

VOL. X
PAGE III

Place	Date	Hour	Summary of Events and Information	Remarks and references to Appendices
POST DUNKERQUE BAINS R.27.c.55.90 Sheet 19 SE	7-10-17		Weather: wind rough, overcast. Gales. Clocks this adopted at 1 a.m. Received S.780 from A.D.M.S. (Unbroken trunks). G.O.C. proceeded on leave from 8/10/17 to 18/10/17 ? During the enemy shell fire attacks we saved at 3 a.m. – 2 trucks, & 1 H.O. broke loose.	HRS
do	8-10-17		Weather: dry & cold. Heavy. A.D.M.S. 41 st Div. visited HRS and inspected Hospital & Camp Arrangements. Authorised Nieuport Bains Shrapnel Dump 182 (D.B. in Estate).	HRS
do	9-10-17		Weather: cols. - bright. 13 cases of opthalmia received from G.O.C. 41 st Div. to 1 Div. NCO's down the half-hour on 20/9/17. Received S.781 from A.D.M.S. (RFA 41 st Div. Gas army)	HRS
do	10-10-17		Weather: cols. - bright. 6. O.R.'s proceeded on leave from 11/10/17 to 27/10/17. Capt R.T. HERDMAN R.A.M.C. + Nursing Brig.S. reported from 41st Stationary hosp. further instructions received from A.D.M.S. 41 st Div. (General Instruction Pamphlets 7 41 st Div.) Received S.782 from A.D.M.S.	HRS
do	11-10-17		Weather: bright. cols. Capt R.T. HERDMAN R.A.M.C. have joined to XV th Corps M.O.S. Sth Army for ao.b. Cellule's week. Received to 35 C.C.Sy 6 from A.D.M.S (139 th F.A) been relieved by 141 st F.A of 139 th Brigade are XV Corps Rawlinson	HRS

WAR DIARY
or
INTELLIGENCE SUMMARY

Army Form C. 2118

13th Bty Vol. X PAGE IV

Place	Date	Hour	Summary of Events and Information	Remarks and references to Appendices
OOST DUNKERKE BAINS R.2.b c.55.76 Sheet VI	12-10-17		Weather bright - wind SW. Received warning order No. 13 from 129th Inf Bde. (Relief of Bde.) 1 Corporal R.A.M.C. arrived from Base as reinforcement. Lt. & Pte. DODDS R.A.M.C. returned from hospital. No arrival rank promotions	WCS
do.	13-10-17		Weather stormy - cold. Entered A.C.S. & ado post at OOST DUNKERKE & advanced R.A.M.P. & also NIEUPORT BAINS. 7 OR returned from front. 9 OR's of Bn went overseas the Ambulancy hospital for gazetting in the field. (Hon't SCRO 2239 d 12/10/17) Received S.783 from A.D.M.S. (Circular Promots) 6. Others of 174 OR admitted during the week & 10 R returned to duty after treatment. Weather high. Memo completed H.Pro - A.D.S OOST DUNKERKE -	WCS
do.	14-10-17		NIEUPORT BAINS & LAITERIE ROYAL 4 OR returned from leave. 6 OR proceeded on leave.	WCS
do.	15-10-17		Hon't Lt. D.A. HORNER OSMORE returned to duty from 19 Middlesex Bn. Lt. J.A. CHARLES R.A.M.C. proceeded to HQS NIEUPORT BAINS to relieve Lt Lt. HOWARD VENTRE who proceeded to this HQ for duty.	WCS
do.	16-10-17		3 OR returned from leave. Ambulances out in France for the construction Secondary General Post C.Hrs. at the Heastgram by H th Ambulance but? Command Received S.783 from A.D.M.S. (Circular (Promotion of Sergeants) Received notification of promotion as Lance Corporal 18/10/17 2 OR returned from leave.	WCS
do.	17-10-17		Weather fair. 6 OR proceeded on Return Steel Helmets etc 1 OR (Corporal) arrived as reinforcement for the base	WCS

WAR DIARY

INTELLIGENCE SUMMARY

138th Field Ambulance

Vol X   Page V

Army Form C. 2118

Place	Date	Hour	Summary of Events and Information	Remarks and references to Appendices
OOST DUNKERKE BAINS. R.27.c.55.26. Sheet XI	19.10.17		Weather very bright. Visited Advanced Post and R.A.P. to make arrangements for the evacuation of flying cases. Item 16 OOST-DUNKERKE. Conveyances are made for re-establishment of new Collecting Post. Capt W. L. WEBSTER. R.A.M.C. posted to its unit but remains attached 4th Army HQ. for temporary duty. 1 O.R. returned from leave.	WS
do	19.10.17		Weather bright and warmer. Received S.785 from A.D.M.S. (opening letter XV Corps Reinforcement Camp.) 1 O.R. (MT ASC) proceeded on 10 days leave 19-29/10 October 1917. 6 O.Rs R.A.M.C. proceeded on 10 days leave from 21-31st October.	WS
do	20.10.17		Weather - bright. 1st Lieut F.C. HOWARD. US. M.O.R.C. returned to 138th F.A. for duty. 1. O.R. (P.B. man attached). Killed at A.D.S NIEUPORT BAINS. S/Cpl. WOODWARD MS returned from A.D.M.S Office for duty and taken on Strength of his unit marking horses to permanent rank. Received S. 786. from A.D.M.S. (location of units).	WS
do	21.10.17		Weather - very bright. 1 O.R. (Cpl.) returned as reinforcement - 2 O.Rs returned back from Lieut Received S 787 from A.D.M.S (correction GTS A B G.O.T No 3)	WS

WAR DIARY or INTELLIGENCE SUMMARY

Army Form C. 2118.

138th Field Ambulance

Vol X. PAGE VI

Place	Date	Hour	Summary of Events and Information	Remarks and references to Appendices
OOST DUNKERKE BAINS Sheet XI R.27.c.55.90.	21.10.17		1st Lieut D.A. HORNER. U.S.M.O.R.C. proceeds to A.D.S. NIEUPORT BAINS for duty. (Additional to Lieut J.A. CHARLES. R.A.M.C.).	WR
do	22.10.17		Weather very bright. Received S.788 from A.D.M.S. (No shelters to be allowed in covered communication trenches beyond Battalion HQ). 30 O.Rs returned from leave. 5 O.Rs proceed on leave 24/10/17 — 3/11/17. Lieut J.A. CHARLES. R.A.M.C. returns to HQ from NIEUPORT BAINS. Received notification of Mr MENDAY as expert on subject. Necessary precautions taken.	WR
do	23.10.17		Weather wet. Capt. J.L.F. LAUDER. D.S.O. M.C. R.H.C. proceeds on leave to England from 24-10-17 — 14-11-17. 1.O.R. returns from leave. 1 FORD Car damaged by fire at Advanced Car Post in OOST DUNKERKE sector. Horse stalling in vicinity of HQ, resultes in direct hit on Sunbeam Ambulance Car, completely disabling it. 1 Ford Car reported for Advanced Car Post. A.A & Q.M.G. visited HQ in connection with establishment of new Trench Foot Centre; duty from 140th F.A. This Car was stationed at Advanced Car Post. FORD Car of 140th F.A. stationed at NIEUPORT BAINS, damaged by	WR
do	24.10.17			WR

Army Form C. 2118.

WAR DIARY
or
INTELLIGENCE SUMMARY

VOL. X PAGE VII

138th Field Ambulance

Place	Date	Hour	Summary of Events and Information	Remarks and references to Appendices
OOST-DUNKERKE BAINS. Sheet XII R.27.c 55.26.	24-10-17		Highland horses near LAITERIE ROYALE. Cos sent to Worccolps for repairs.	WRS
do.	25.10.17		Weather very wet 6 ORS proceeded on leave from 27-10-17 — 6/11/17. Proceeded with D.A.D.M.S to OOST-DUNKERKE and Advanced Cas Post. Headquarters visited by G.O.C 41st Division. Received S.786 from A.D.M.S (Locature of Divisional huts). Received S 789 from A.D.M.S (Officiateur 2nd ARMY Officiant YPRES Salient.) 1 Sunbeam Ambulance Car arriving for ensuring duty from 139th F.A. Trench foot Stations.	WRS
do.	27.10.17		Extra pontine trenches in respect day and night. Weather fine and bright.	WRS
do.	28.10.17		Orders A.D.S.s and outposts Trench foot Centre for inspection of hygiene. Weather very bright. Received A.D.M.S. 41st Division. Letters and 2 p/s overale A.D.S. and HQ and returned to TETEGHEM area. Advance party from 28th F.A. arrived at noon and relief commenced. Transport proceeded to TETEGHEM Area (Sheet 19. I 6 a.29.5) by march route. Relief completed by 10.30 P.M. Advance party of Arts F.A. proceeded to COXYDE BAINS for embussing at 4 P.M. Remainder proceeded at 11 P.M for embussing at same point and arrived at TETEGHEM at 4.30 A.M on 29.10.17. Received Operation Order	WRS

Army Form C. 2118.

WAR DIARY
or
INTELLIGENCE SUMMARY

(Erase heading not required.)

138th Field Ambulance Vol. X PAGE VIII

Instructions regarding War Diaries and Intelligence Summaries are contained in F. S. Regs., Part II. and the Staff Manual respectively. Title Pages will be prepared in manuscript.

Place	Date	Hour	Summary of Events and Information	Remarks and references to Appendices
OOST. DUNKERKE BM1n8. Sheet 51. R.27.c.55.2.6.	28-10-17		35 a.m. from A.D.M.S. in conjunction of orders verbally received in the morning. Received Brigade warning orders. No 15. from 122 Brigade. Co. little or no prior to commencement of move Capt R.T. HERDMAN and two other ranks proceeded to TETEGHEM area at 1 P.M.	WRH
OXELM Sheet XIX. I.6.a.2.9.	29.10.17		Location of unit reported to A.D.M.S. and Brigade HQ at 10 A.M. Arrangements made for the collection of the sick of the Brigade. All Officers and men of the Unit on leave orders to rejoin immediately. Capt. W. L. WEBSTER. R.A.M.C. transferred to 9th Division, and taken eft strength of this unit. (Authority. A.D.M.S. S.25.00) Received S.790 from A.D.M.S. (Equipment required to complete was established in due to be indented for, and Officers and Mens kit to be reduced to recognised winter scale.).	WRH
DO.	30.10.17		Weather very wet. Capt R.T. HERDMAN transferred to A.D.M.S. 42nd Division for duty in accordance with instructions A.D.M.S. 41st Division (M. 1/16 dated 30.10.17). Received S.791 from A.D.M.S (41st Division was being dismantled.).	WRH

2449 Wt. W14957/M90 750,000 1/16 J.B.C. & A. Forms/C.2118/12.

WAR DIARY
or
INTELLIGENCE SUMMARY

Army Form C. 2118.

198th Field Ambulance Vol X. Page IX

Place	Date	Hour	Summary of Events and Information	Remarks and references to Appendices
OXEM Sheet XIX I.6.a.29.	31.10.17		Weather bright. Attended conference at A.D.M.S. Office at 11 A.M. Full issue of Jerseys held and all clothing and equipment inspected, this operation being perfect. Received one Ford and one Sunbeam ambulance to replace 2 motor ambulances damaged by hostile shell fire. Strength of unit at end of month — Officers: two detached on leave. Other Ranks: eight in hospital, otherwise War Establishment complete.	MCS

31/10/17

Wm Grant Lt Col
R.A.M.C.
O.C. 198th Field Ambulance.

www.ingramcontent.com/pod-product-compliance
Lightning Source LLC
Chambersburg PA
CBHW081542160426
43191CB00011B/1821